IN BUT STILL OUT

"I told them I'm enchanted, and they believed. I told them I'm a good, Christian woman, and they believed. I told them I'm a God-fearing, Bible-quoting, volunteering, Presbyterian elder, and they believed. Then I told them I wanted power in the church, and they called me a toad."

76586

IN BUT STILL OUT

WOMEN IN THE CHURCH

Elizabeth Howell Verdesi

THE WESTMINSTER PRESS
PHILADELPHIA

COPYRIGHT © 1973 AND 1976 ELIZABETH HOWELL VERDESI

All rights reserved—no part of this book may be reproduced in any form without permission in writing from the publisher, except by a reviewer who wishes to quote brief passages in connection with a review in magazine or newspaper.

BOOK DESIGN BY DOROTHY E. JONES

PUBLISHED BY THE WESTMINSTER PRESS ®
PHILADELPHIA, PENNSYLVANIA

PRINTED IN THE UNITED STATES OF AMERICA

Library of Congress Cataloging in Publication Data

Verdesi, Elizabeth Howell, 1922–
   In but still out.

   Based on the author's thesis, Columbia University and Union Theological Seminary, New York, 1975.
   Bibliography: p.
   1. Women in church work—Presbyterian Church.
I. Title.
BV4415.V45 1976   253'.2   75-34365
ISBN 0-664-24788-1

Contents

PREFACE		7
ACKNOWLEDGMENTS		13
	1. Encounter in the Seventies	15
PART ONE		35
	2. Benevolence Dressed in Female Form	37
	3. "The Women That Publish the Tidings Are a Great Host"	55
	4. Aftermath and the Drive for Equality	79
PART TWO		109
	5. "Both Men and Women May Be Called to This Office"	113

6.	The Rise and Fall of a Power Base	138
7.	"In Christ There Is Neither Male nor Female" . . . But in the Presbyterian Church?	160

APPENDIX: Note on Women's Power in the Church   183

NOTES   187

SELECTED BIBLIOGRAPHY   209

Preface

In one sense, this study began the day I was born. Carried to church in a laundry basket, I soon became aware that for both my mother and father, and indeed for many of my relatives, church activities provided the core of their lives. Not that any of them were ordained as ministers or professional church workers. Rather, they were the kind of concerned, capable, and dependable lay leaders that every minister wishes all his members would be but too often are not.

So it was not unusual that I attended church and Sunday school regularly, sat next to the pastor every Wednesday at Family Night Suppers, sang in the choir, took part in plays and programs—even to the point of helping organize the "Bloomer Girls," a motley group of teen-agers. Part of growing up in the church also meant attending summer conferences at Wells College, Aurora, New York, where I learned to balance upstanding comportment with a dash of deviltry.

It was there that I was exposed to the idea that I, Elizabeth Howell, might actually serve the church. Since age seven, I had been determined to be a surgeon. Marriage, home, family—these were not the stuff of my dreams. Fame, money, with some measure of "doing good" thrown in—these were my dreams. But at Aurora, the values inherent in those dreams seemed shabby somehow, superficial. Near the close of my last conference, I felt God's presence—no vision, no voice—just a kind of powerful presence that seemed to envelop me and made me feel whole, wanted, and waiting.

From that time on, I knew that I wanted to serve the church. In great detail I worked on various plans for my life—missionary doctor, missionary teacher, teaching doctor, and so forth. Not that plans like that ever work out. But making those plans gave me a drive and a direction.

Before, when people responded to my declaration about wanting to be a surgeon with the customary, "Oh, you mean you want to be a nurse?" I was always angered. In much the same way, I felt anger, bitterness, and hurt because I could not even consider being a minister of my church. Whatever my talents and abilities, limitations and weaknesses—because I was a girl I would have to become either a missionary or a Christian educator.

About this time (1938), a new status for women was established by the General Assembly, that of commissioned church worker. I could not understand why this was necessary. Why *couldn't* women just be ordained as ministers? One day I met a woman minister of the Congregational church, and my mother told me how our presbytery had actually ordained her once, back in World War I, but the synod had found her ordination illegal and she had been barred from further work in the Presbyterian Church.

Almost thirty years passed—years in which I had several outstanding opportunities to serve the church professionally. First as a "Traveling Fellow" for the Board of Christian Education for one year—to do recruiting of young people for church vocations. (Ironically, I was considered capable of recruiting future ministers but not capable of being one!) Then six years as a "Board secretary," Secretary for Youth Work of the Board of National Missions, in which I traveled all over the United States, speaking, writing, leading seminars and workshops, helping to set policy and plan curriculum. Eventually I married a Presbyterian pastor, and learned what it is like to be a minister's wife, as well as a presbyterial and synodical officer, and director of Christian education in a local church. Later on, I became a ruling elder, active in presbytery committees, and full circle again, I am serving as a member of the professional staff of Church Women United in the U.S.A.

When it came time for me to select my dissertation topic, I cast about in a variety of directions. The

women's liberation movement was beginning to stir—
and something inside me began to stir also. I thought
about writing a simple history of how women in the
Presbyterian Church were first recognized as missionaries, then as Christian educators, and finally as
ordained ministers. It was to be a straightforward
description of changing roles. Even though I had a
long background of interest and work related to
Presbyterian Women, I felt that I must focus the
dissertation very sharply on the professional woman,
lest I get bogged down in a mire of fascinating but
irrelevant history.

But I failed to reckon with history! One day as I
was looking over some historical materials in the New
York offices of United Presbyterian Women, I came
across a small notebook with pages falling out of it.
Inside was information that definitively linked the
story of Presbyterian laywomen and professional
women. The most startling paper was a copy of a 1929
telegram from the Stated Clerk of the General Assembly to some members of the General Council, requesting verification of their vote against sending to the
presbyteries an overture that would have permitted
the ordination of women. Why should such a telegram
be in the archives of Presbyterian Women? There
were other memos there too, and by piecing some of
them together, I began to glimpse the link that needed
to be uncovered.

For the next months I became engrossed in the
whole history of what Presbyterian women had done
in the nineteenth century. Only so could I understand

the trauma experienced by the women when the General Assembly voted in 1922 to reorganize all the boards and agencies of the denomination, including their own Woman's Board of Home Missions. As I studied the various documents of the 1920's, I became acutely aware that the entire drama was in fact a kind of power play in a game that the women lost.

As a Christian educator and commissioned church worker myself, I had long been concerned with the dwindling leadership of women in the religious education field. The more I hypothesized about the women's loss of power in the 1920's, the more convinced I was that something similar had happened with religious educators, many of whom were known to me personally in the 1940's and 1950's.

To discover what that something was, and more important, what happens between men and women—both individually and institutionally—between those in power and those not in power—all this started me on a search that will probably continue until the day I die!

E.H.V.

Acknowledgments

This work has come into its present form by the aid of uncounted persons who have helped in small acts of accommodations as well as in larger measures of assistance and sharing. To all of these persons, too numerous to name here, my sincere thanks.

Basic material for this book was first presented as a doctoral dissertation for my work at Teachers College, Columbia University, and Union Theological Seminary in New York. To my advisers, Dr. Hope Leichter and Dr. Philip Phenix, whose affirming interest and openness never flagged, my continuing appreciation. Particularly to Dr. Robert W. Lynn, my sponsor, whose patient probing and enthusiastic encouragement truly "enabled" this work, my deepest respect, admiration, and thanks.

These words of acknowledgment, however, would not be complete without special mention of the contributions that others have made to this project: the Rev. Alan G. Gripe, whose original encouragement and sharing of information and contacts were invaluable; the executive director of Church Women United in the U.S.A., Margaret Shannon, who permitted me to take time for the later stages of writing; Eleanor Bryce, Betsy Garland, Maria Martinez, and Dana Simone, who willingly spent long hours and much energy in typing the manuscript with diligence, accuracy, and devotion; to Betsy Garland and Ruth Weber, whose editing has helped to make the reading clear; my sons, Stephen and David, whose understanding over the years often rekindled my own commitment; and my husband, the Rev. Ariel Verdesi, who has been unfailing in his support. To all of these, my everlasting gratitude.

1

ENCOUNTER IN THE SEVENTIES

Poised and petite, modishly dressed, with silvery hair, she stood in dignity before the assembly. The place was the Community War Memorial Auditorium in Rochester, New York; the date, May 25, 1971. The first woman Moderator of the General Assembly of The United Presbyterian Church in the U.S.A. said firmly but warmly, "Defeat is bitter enough without having it applauded and laughed at." [1]

Her gentle reprimand was directed toward the 749 commissioners (ruling elders and ministers), convened for the 183d annual meeting of the denomination. They had just clapped and tittered over the defeat of a motion that had come at the end of the Report of the Standing Committee on Women. Mrs. Lois Stair of Waukesha, Wisconsin, had been elected Moderator a few days before by a bare majority of twelve votes. Stepping to the microphone to resume presiding after the report, Mrs. Stair spoke in the tense atmosphere that had developed while the Vice-Moderator, Dr. John Thompson Peters of Toledo, Ohio (her closest opponent in the election), was chairing the Assembly.

The Standing Committee on Women had worked from a Report of the Special Task Force on Women, appointed in 1969 by the 181st General Assembly to study the status and role of women in the church. There had been much debate, some of it rancorous and patronizing, throughout the report.[2] Then, at the conclusion of the report, a man and a woman, both members of the Task Force on Women, requested permission to read "A Confession," signed by sixty-nine men and women. The substance of the Confession was a listing of the ways in which men have abused their power over women, seeing them mainly as sex objects; and a summary of the ways in which women have failed to fulfill their own potentialities as human beings. The two ended the reading of this Confession with a motion that the self-accusing signers be referred to the Permanent Judicial Commission for censure. As this motion was read, the commissioners sat stunned, disbelieving. A few chuckles of embarrassment were heard. Even the Vice-Moderator, who had been asked by Mrs. Stair to preside for this part of the meeting, was unsure how to proceed. When assured by the confessors that they were in earnest, he put the motion to the Assembly. It was quickly voted down. In their embarrassment and relief, many of the commissioners laughed and applauded.

It was at this moment that Mrs. Stair stepped forward and made her statement. Herself a member of the Task Force on Women, out of which had come the Confession, she knew how deeply the confessors felt about what they had written. She remembered too the snickering and the nudges among the male commissioners in the afternoon when they spotted a large group of women in the gallery.[3] About sixty women had come to Rochester for a meeting of the Women's Caucus. Many of them were professionally trained— ordained ministers, commissioned church workers, and Christian educators. For them it was a moment of revelation in which the church's attitude toward and treatment of women had been quintessentially demonstrated. All the years of controversy about women's right to ordination as elders and ministers, all the debates about Scriptural proscriptions against women's leadership in the church, all the subtle and not-so-subtle put-downs endured by women over the years, and somehow all the energies poured out by women in study and fund-raising and teaching were caught up and symbolized in that moment.[4]

Women in the Presbyterian Church had come a long way. Among major denominations, The United Presbyterian Church in the U.S.A. is one of the few in which women in the past seventy years moved from having *no* status, except as church members, to full ecclesiastical equality. Recognition of this equality was finally made with the election of Lois Stair as Moderator of the General Assembly in 1971.

In analyzing the experience at General Assembly in Rochester, a number of women became aware that two things had happened: First, many women, especially professional women in the church, had been "radicalized" by the treatment that the Report of the Standing Committee on Women had received. Second, women still had much to learn about how to get things done in the church.[5] The first effect was mainly personal and individual. But the second had to do with political astuteness and the uses of power. Women had been made aware that the church is caught in the same kinds of cultural binds as is society. It responds more readily to power effectively used and to political savoir faire than it does to just causes or to obvious commitment.[6]

The issue of power for women in this Presbyterian denomination has always been a difficult one. At various points in its history women have attained real power. But when this has happened, somehow the women have lost it to the institutional power structure. Whenever women have had access to power, they have made advances toward full equality in the church. But an effective, continuing share in power has eluded them. By 1956 women achieved full ecclesiastical status by being permitted ordination to the ministry. But nineteen years later, in 1975, there are still only about 190 ordained women ministers out of a total of over 13,000 ministers in this denomination.

And of these, only about 20 have pastorates of their own.

There are dimensions in this situation which defy easy analysis. Some are cultural, some are economic, some are psychological. But these dimensions must be explored if women are ever to be free to make their full contribution to the church.

Where Did All the Power Go?

The purpose of this book is to show what has happened in the Presbyterian Church when women have secured a power base for themselves, and in particular, how this power base has affected the achievement of status and equality by women trained for professional service in the church. *The notion that will be developed and documented is this: In the two instances in the twentieth century when women established a power base in the Presbyterian Church, the reality and effectiveness of that power base was lost through the process of co-optation, and as a result, professionally trained women have been hindered in achieving full equality in the church.* It will also be shown that the development of the power base in each instance depended on the good offices and assistance of certain men who had access to power in the church, and that the loss of power was not necessarily motivated by any conscious intent on the part of either men or women.

The development of this idea depends on an

understanding of the efforts made by some women in the church to attain full ecclesiastical status. Succeeding chapters will explore the roots of the movement for equality in the voluntary organizations of laywomen in the church. The first instance of the establishment of a power base involved the Woman's Board of Home Missions, a voluntary organization of laywomen. From the loss of this power base came the first organized effort to achieve full *ecclesiastical* equality. Therefore, the background of this lay organization in nineteenth-century feminism will also be considered.

The second instance occurred in relation to the religious education movement within the Presbyterian Church. This development will highlight some of the events in the twentieth century that have brought ecclesiastical recognition to women, including ordination to the ministry. It will also analyze the effects that changes in status have brought to the work and experience of professionally trained women.

This study is concerned only with the Presbyterian Church in the U.S.A. up to 1958, and since then with The United Presbyterian Church in the U.S.A., the denomination produced through merger of the former Presbyterian Church in the U.S.A. and the United Presbyterian Church of North America. It will focus on those women who, since 1938, the first year that General Assembly recognized professional women in the church, have served the denomination in the continental United States only. The major reason for setting such a limitation is that the qualifications, role, opportunities, and experience of women sent overseas as missionaries have largely been determined by the culture and demands of the countries where they have worked. The experiences of those women are somewhat different and of minimal relevance to the concerns of this study.

Clarifying Concepts

Power Base—What Is It?

By one dictionary definition, "power" is (1) the "possession of control, authority, or influence over others" [7] or (2) the ability to act or produce an effect. The word "base" is defined as a foundation or supporting structure and may refer to "anything upon which a structure is built and upon which it rests." [8] The phrase "power base" will be used here to denote "a source of authority or influence" [9] and will refer to the organized group that possesses both authority and the ability to act.

Professionally Trained Women—Who Are They?

As an institution, the church employs women in a variety of jobs—as nurses, social workers, doctors, and administrators on the mission field; as ministers, assistant ministers, directors of Christian education, secretaries, and sometimes even cooks in local churches; as bookkeepers, clerks, executives, and administrative assistants in its agencies. From the standpoint of personnel categories, any one of these require "professionally trained women."

In the case of a missionary nurse or teacher, or a

church social worker, or a minister of music, however, while she or he may be working professionally in the church, her or his *standing as a professional* in her or his field is determined, not by the church, but by an examining board or licensing agency or some other group of colleagues in that profession.

For this reason, the term "professionally trained woman" will, for the purposes of this study, be used to designate *only* those women who have *ecclesiastical standing* in the church. This means that their credentials and certification for that standing are *determined by the General Assembly,* and that their employment is administered under the jurisdiction of a judicatory beyond the local church (i.e., presbytery, synod, or General Assembly). Such a definition includes then only ordained ministers, commissioned church workers, and certified church educators.

Co-optation—What Does It Mean?

In *TVA and the Grass Roots*, Philip Selznick defines co-optation as "the process of absorbing new elements into the leadership or policy-determining structure of an organization as a means of averting threats to its stability or existence." [10] This study contends that a *process of co-optation* has operated in the Presbyterian Church whenever women have gained substantive power.

Mr. Selznick makes a distinction between "formal" and "informal" co-optation. In the formal process, an organization publicly acknowledges its need to recognize new elements through appointments to official positions, through inclusion of representatives on policy committees, or through establishing a new organization. Basically, these efforts are "showcase" maneuvers, designed to lower the pressure from the threatening group. Formal co-optation "does not envision the transfer of actual power." [11] The co-opting group provides participation for the new element but manages to maintain the decision-making power in its own hands. An organization makes use of formal co-optation under either of two conditions: (1) when the legitimacy of its authority is challenged or (2) when the administration of a particular program is so precarious that a form of self-governing becomes advisable. An example of the first instance occurs when one of the leaders of a dissenting minority is made a member of the governing group in power. Recent history furnishes multiple examples of this kind of co-optation: i.e., the British placing Indians in government posts; universities appointing student dissidents to policy-making committees; government agencies hiring black leaders as administrators. An example of the second condition is seen when the administrators of a housing project organize a committee of residents to prevent vandalism, or the head of a prison establishes a committee of prisoners to ensure obedience to regulations.

Informal co-optation, on the other hand, is the response of an organization to certain individuals or pressure groups that have the leverage to *enforce* their demands, according to Selznick.[12] In cases of informal co-optation, open surrender to such pressures might undermine the authority of the organization. Consequently, these special interest groups are permitted to exercise their power informally, as in a political party. The pressure groups are satisfied with this arrangement, since they are more concerned with the exercise of actual power than with its forms.[13]

This simply means that co-optation effects a change in the organization, and this results in a dilemma: how to provide sufficient participation in the organization to satisfy the co-opted elements without losing control.

The word "co-opted" is in wide usage in Presbyterian and other ecclesiastical circles, but usually its meaning is limited to the dictionary definition, i.e., choosing or electing someone as a fellow member or colleague. Rarely, if ever, is it used in connection with organizational behavior. But for the purpose of this presentation, the terms "co-opted" and "co-optation" will refer solely to organizational behavior. The study will show that the loss of the power base was brought about through formal co-optation. In the first instance, the power vested in the Woman's Board of Home Missions was needed by the larger church structures. Consequently, the women's power base was co-opted through reorganization. In the second instance, legitimization was sought by the women in the religious education movement. As a result, they co-opted men into leadership roles and then lost control of the movement. Both events noticeably influenced the struggle for status and equality for professionally trained women.

The Professionally Trained Woman in the Presbyterian Church

Before developing this theory, it is essential to outline briefly the present plight of professionally trained women so that the significance and relevance of this study can be understood.

Women in the Presbyterian Church finally overcame the last barrier to full ecclesiastical equality in 1956, when the General Assembly approved the ordination of women to the ministry. This was done by the addition of a simple sentence to the Form of Government (Ch. VII, Sec. 2): "Both men and women may be called to this office." It had taken eighty-four years from the time when the question about ordaining women was first brought to the General Assembly. The issue was then addressed in a strikingly negative way. In 1872 the Presbytery of Brooklyn overtured the Assembly as follows:

> that the Assembly accept and transmit to the presbyteries for their approval such rules as shall forbid the licensing and ordaining of women to the gospel ministry, and the teaching and preaching of women in our pulpits, or in the public and promiscuous meetings of the Church of Christ.[14]

Reliable statistics about the number of women ministers in the Presbyterian denomination are difficult to obtain, since no separate count was kept until 1970. However, the 1960 report from General Assembly shows 24. Ten years later the number had increased to

76. There were 103 in 1971, and 120 by 1972. The latest count (1975) indicates 189. While this increase during the past triennium has been rapid, the question still remains: *Why* are there so few women ministers out of a total of 13,000—after 19 years? And of these, why do so few hold pastorates of their own? Are women just not interested in the ministry as a profession? Are they not capable of fulfilling the responsibilities of the pastoral office? Or, is it possible that, knowing the obstacles involved in securing and keeping significant ministerial positions, they prefer to prepare for other types of work? Or are churches, accustomed to male pastors, unwilling to call women ministers?

To secure answers to some of these questions, the Task Force on Women sent a detailed questionnaire to all women ministers late in 1969. The replies from this survey corroborate the observations made by Kenneth G. McCullough in a paper written for the Task Force. In analyzing the employment records of the women ministers in the United Presbyterian Church, he found that ordained women employment records showed a lack of mobility:

> The largest percentage of them first took a position as assistant pastor. A relatively small number advanced to the status of associate pastor, and only one became pastor of the church she originally served as assistant pastor.[15]

Comparing the record of all the ordained women with the employment record of a control group of male ministers, he also discovered that women are more likely to be unemployed and more likely to give up a church occupation than their male colleagues. On the basis of his study, McCullough concluded that "no recommendation of General Assembly will remove the causes of frustration of these female human beings in the dynamic situation in which they would hope to serve." [16]

Typical of this frustration is the letter received by a woman in 1971 while she was waiting for a "call" so that she could be ordained. (In the United Presbyterian Church no person may now be ordained until he or she has a "call" to a specific position.) With a seminary degree and a master's degree, and with her doctoral dissertation almost completed, she was experienced, capable, and well recommended. But when her dossier was sent by the Department of Ministerial Relations to a church seeking an assistant pastor, she received a letter from the chairman of the nominating committee of that church, which read in part as follows:

> The nominating committee has considered your dossier along with others. However, since we have a female staff person at present, the committee will not be considering you for this position. We appreciate greatly the privilege of considering you.[17]

On the letterhead was listed a pastor, an associate pastor, and a minister of music—all male, and a director of Christian education who was female. Apparently *one woman* on the staff precluded the consideration of another qualified woman—even though *three men* on the staff did not prevent their plan to hire a fourth.

But the ordained woman minister is not the only professionally trained woman who finds frustration in the church. The commissioned church worker has faced continuing problems ever since the status was approved in 1938 by the General Assembly. This was the first action establishing qualifications and certification procedures for which women were eligible. Since then, commissioning has been chosen by many women who wished to serve professionally in the church, usually as directors of Christian education. This status is open to men also.

At this point, some statistics may be helpful. In the period between 1960 and 1969, General Assembly records show the following:[18]

	1960	*1964*	*1969*
Churches	9,353	9,100	8,667
Ministers	12,216	12,618	13,201
Men	12,192	12,567	13,125
Women	24	51	76
Commissioned church workers	223	217	161
Men	23	25	26
Women	200	192	135

This table shows that the number of women commissioned church workers steadily declined during the '60s, while the number of men in this category remained almost constant. The chart also indicates that the *total* number of professionally trained women (ordained and commissioned)—in spite of the increase in the number of women ministers—*declined* from .018 percent of the total in 1960 to .015 percent in 1969. With an unknown number of the women commissioned church workers not employed in the denomination at present (the author being one), and with only 20 out of the 35 ordained respondents to the Task Force survey working in church-related jobs in 1969, it is evident that the number of professionally trained women actually working today in the Presbyterian Church is infinitesimal.

Fewer Jobs in the Church

In the fall of 1971, the Division of Vocation of the Board of Christian Education prepared a report on "The Professional Ministry of the United Presbyterian Church," based on data from the previous decade. According to this report, the factors determining the need for professional personnel are: *(a)* salaries, *(b)* vacancies, *(c)* the number of communicant members in the church, and *(d)* the benevolence giving of the church. The report points out that there has been a "distinct rise in the average salaries of ministers," [19] but that the number of vacant churches is not a reliable index to the demand for ministers, since the number of churches without pastors that are able to pay an adequate salary is very low.[20]

Concerning the ratio of communicant members to active ordained ministers, the report shows a change from 317 to 1 in 1960 to 291 to 1 in 1970. This may mean that a "cleaning of the rolls" has taken place, or it may mean that personnel procedures "are improving." [21]

The most startling note in the report concerned ordained women ministers and candidates. In one year (1970) the number of ordained women ministers jumped from 76 to 103.[22] Even more surprising is the fact that, according to the records, in 1971 there were 213 women ministerial candidates in seminaries, 72 of whom were planning to go into the gospel ministry, and 71 into other areas.[23]

Not only are there more women entering the ministry, but the Department of Ministerial Relations reported that in the first six months of 1970, 142 women candidates had been added to their files, and in 1971 during the same period, 258 candidates were added.[24]

This report makes it obvious that while the supply of ordained ministers, especially women, is increasing, the demand for ordained ministers—either male or female—is steadily decreasing.

There is also other information pertinent to the discussion about the plight of the professional woman in the church. According to a report prepared by the Division of Vocation there were 291 directors of Christian education in 1963, and 207 in 1967. (Figures for 1971 are unavailable because of computer malfunction.) By contrast, the number of "assistants in Christian education" increased markedly: 290 in 1963 and 333 in 1967.[25] This is significant because the title

"Director of Christian Education" usually designates someone who has had graduate study in a seminary (often with a master's degree), whereas "Assistant in Christian Education" is used somewhat loosely by congregations for whoever is paid to work in the Christian education program. Sometimes assistants in Christian education have a bachelor's degree with a major in Bible, religion, or religious education. Sometimes they have had no formal higher education, but do have extensive training and experience in the Christian education field. In any case, the assistants do not qualify as "professionally trained," according to the definition given above.

These statistics mean that the number of professionally trained personnel in Christian education positions, mostly women, declined by almost one third between 1963 and 1967, while the number of nonprofessionals steadily increased.[26]

In summary, it is apparent that the ordained woman can find herself frustrated by discrimination in many shapes and forms. The commissioned woman may find herself caught in the "job-money squeeze," since qualified, trained directors always command a higher salary than do nonprofessionally trained assistants. At a time in history when women are being catapulted into prominence in politics, in business, and in the media, here stands a coterie of women—trained for work in the church—who find themselves unwanted and who face unemployment. It should be noted, however, that this situation is not limited to women.

With the recent restructuring and decentralizing of the Presbyterian Church many professionally trained men have been facing the same prospect.

Women's Liberation and the Church

With women's consciousness-raising groups meeting all across the nation, and with the media capitalizing on the impact of the women's revolution in America, the church has come in for its share of attack during the past several years. The women's liberation movement, therefore, has been a factor in shaping this inquiry.

For many years the role of women in the church has been a subject of controversy and concern. One conference in 1951, chaired by Professor Ursula Niebuhr of Barnard College, brought together professors, clergymen, graduate students—both men and women —to consider "Women and the Church." A report of that conference, written by Betty M. Rice, concluded that

> secular culture, with its admittance of women on an equal basis into most walks of life, has advanced far beyond the church community.[27]

Soon after Betty Friedan published her best-selling book, *The Feminine Mystique*, the magazine published by the Chicago City Mission Society, entitled *Renewal*, devoted its entire October 1964 issue to the subject of women and the church. In it, the Rev. Peggy Way, formerly a professor at Chicago Theological Seminary, wrote:

> It is a fact that formal Church leadership (need we state that it is predominantly male?) has counted on the women to raise money *in whatever ways they could;* to do "good works" *for the entire Church;* and to keep themselves occupied in their own organizations and *out of the sessions, vestries, church councils, presbyteries, etc.—where the real decisions concerning the Church are made.* . . . Popular and serious literature has for some time now been re-evaluating the role of women in the contemporary world. The Church has been singularly silent.[28]

She also commented on the situation of the professionally trained woman, as follows:

> It is time to say openly that the Church treats its own professionally trained women, its Christian educators and pastors, as second-class citizens. If this is so, it is no wonder that women's groups have followed the directions they have taken. The recently passed legislation assuring "equal pay for equal work" for women will be embarrassing to no organization more than the Church.[29]

Three years later, Doris Cole, wife of the president of Lake Forest College in Illinois, and herself an elder in a local Presbyterian church, reiterated the charge that women are "second-class" in the May issue of *Vanguard*, a bulletin for church officers published by the Board of Christian Education.[30]

These were voices of women "crying in the wilderness." Some of these voices, augmented by many more, have been heard over the years of this century. By mid-century (1956 to be exact) the Presbyterian Church, unlike many other denominations, had altered its Constitution so that women could be accorded equal status with men at every level of ecclesiastical life.

Looking back on the past, however, one can see a paradox: In spite of the full ecclesiastical equality now legally open to women in the Presbyterian Church, generally they are not equally part of the power structures of the church. Moreover, professionally trained women are continuing to find it difficult to obtain and retain positions that are commensurate with their education and experience.

To discover how this paradox has developed and why, this book will explore some of those forces and events in the past that have shaped the present. It is a presupposition that a thorough understanding of the past is prerequisite to significant work in the present and to planning for the future. Examining those forces and events of the past may enable Presbyterian women to move into the last decades of the twentieth century, not only as the ecclesiastical equals of men but as more effective servants of the church.

The achievement of full ecclesiastical equality for women in the Presbyterian Church has been a long struggle fraught with frustration and complexity. Often the role of power in that development has gone unrecognized. From the telling of this story, however, we may learn that to achieve status and equality does not guarantee a proportionate share of power. That struggle still goes on.

PART ONE

To understand the role of power in attaining equality for women in the Presbyterian Church, a look must first be taken at the power base the women themselves had established, and whose co-optation in 1923 led them to demand equality. Such a look involves understanding the origin, development, nature, and work of the Woman's Board of Home Missions, and its relation to the rest of the church at the time.

And so the story begins with the "pious and benevolent females" of the early 1800's . . .

2

BENEVOLENCE DRESSED IN FEMALE FORM

> Benevolence is always attractive, but when dressed in female form, possesses peculiar charms. . . . We hope the spirit which has animated the worthy women of whom we speak, will spread and animate other bosoms.[1]
>
> *"Minutes of the General Assembly," 1811*

Women in nineteenth-century America were stirring. Some of them moved west with their families to set up new homes on the frontier. Some discovered their own voices, which they used to speak out against slavery. Some remained in the East, but sent prayers and money and boxes to those on the frontier. This is part of the stirring story of what some Presbyterian women in the East did for the frontier—and for future generations of women.

Voluntary groups of American women, formed to give continuity to their concerns, had their origins in the early years of the nineteenth century. These groups have been called unique in the Western world. One of the first avenues open to such women's organizations was the church.[2] Apparently the men of the church appreciated the work of these early women's groups, as evidenced by the Minutes of the General Assembly in 1811 noted above. It is much less certain that the men took any part in opening up these avenues for the women. From the meager records that are still available, it appears that these groups sprang up spontaneously on the initiative of the women themselves. Sometimes they came together under the wary eye of the men, especially the clergy. One minister, after opening their meeting with prayer (since women were not permitted to pray in public at this time), was invited by the ladies to leave. He declined, explaining, "No one knew what they would pray for if left alone." [3]

The first organization of Presbyterian women of which there is record was founded in 1803. Related to the First Presbyterian Church of Newark, New Jersey, it was known as the Female Charitable Society. The particular impetus that gave rise to the organization of this society is not clear. But two years after its inception, the pastor of the church, Dr. MacWhorter, commented in a sermon:

This society was "instituted for the most benevolent purposes, and it is allowed by all that they have done much good. . . . Their charity has been judicially and frugally expended. None, as far as I know, have reflected upon them, or blamed them, but multitudes have spoken much in their praise."[4]

The existence of other such organizations at this time is evidenced by the request of Gideon Blackburn, the first Presbyterian missionary to work with the Cherokee Indians in Tennessee. In 1806 he wrote to Dr. Ashbel Green, chairman of General Assembly's Standing Committee on Home Missions, "Ask your Female Societies to pray for me and my little Indians."[5]

These societies took a variety of names: Female Cent Society, Female Praying Society, Female Home Missionary Society, Female Bible Society, Female Mite Society, Female Dollar Society, and so on.[6] The name of their society apparently reflected both the purpose of their organization and the focus of their concern, and in some cases, the affluence of their members!

The Good Works of Pious and Benevolent Females

In the early years the "pious and benevolent females" seem to have been more concerned about those who were *doing* the ministering on the frontier than about those who were being ministered to. From the records, it appears that their benevolence was directed toward three concerns: (1) the pioneer Sunday school workers on the frontier; (2) "pious and indigent" ministerial students; and (3) missionaries such as Blackburn.[7] During the first half of the nineteenth century the women served as a kind of auxiliary group, working to assist the mission projects and personnel that had been established and that were administered by the men of the church. Later, this focus was to shift as the women began to initiate mission work on their own, which they then supported and administered.

During the 1820's and 1830's these missionary societies proliferated throughout New York and Pennsylvania. Others were formed as far south and west as Virginia and what is now West Virginia. In fact, the number of Presbyterian women's groups, whose records are still extant, doubled from 45 in 1820 to 91 in 1840, with 17 more added in the next 13 years.[8] These women were not only "pious and benevolent"; they were also capable and industrious. With their mites and their dollars, with their needles, books, and pin cushions, with their tracts and their prayers, they were quite unknowingly preparing the stage for other concerns. The movement for women's rights and the abolition of slavery would soon erupt into controversy and war.

New Causes for Nineteenth-Century Women—Rights and Abolition

The sensitivities of some women in the 1840's and 1850's were galvanized by the controversy over abolition. They soon discovered that sincerity in support of abolition was not a sufficient qualification for full participation in the cause. This was made dramatically clear to the eight women who traveled to London in 1840 as part of the American delegation to the World Anti-Slavery Convention. Among them were Lucretia Mott, ardent abolitionist, and Elizabeth Cady Stanton, bride of the abolitionist leader, Henry Stanton. In spite of the objections of the American contingent, the convention ruled that the women could not be seated as delegates.[9] This was a traumatic experience for Mrs. Stanton, who, for the rest of her life, along with many other women, poured her energies into the movement for women's rights.

During the years of turmoil in the latter part of the nineteenth century, where were the "pious and benevolent females" of the Presbyterian churches? Were they involved in the new movements? Or were they content to continue their sewing and saving in silence, satisfied that in this way they could serve best?

It is difficult, if not impossible, to establish any direct relationship between the activities of Presbyterian women and the movement for women's rights. According to Florence Hayes, in her sesquicentennial history of women's work in the Presbyterian Church, *Daughters of Dorcas*, there is "no evidence that the members of the early female societies took active part in any of these woman's movements." [10]

One exception may be Matilda Joslyn Gage, who was one of the less famous but more capable early feminists—and a Presbyterian!

In the *Dictionary of American Biography*, she is described as follows:

> Intellectually she was without doubt among the ablest of the suffrage leaders of the nineteenth century. An excellent speaker and capable organizer, her greatest strength apparently lay in her thorough grasp of the historical status of women through the ages.[11]

Elizabeth Cady Stanton said that "she always had a knack of rummaging through old libraries bringing more startling facts to light than any woman I ever knew." [12]

Born in Cicero, New York, in 1826 into a doctor's family, Matilda was taught Greek, physiology, and mathematics by her father, who was interested in reform movements and made his home the intellectual center of town. After attending Clinton Seminary, at age eighteen she married a merchant and moved with him to Syracuse, Manlius, and finally Fayetteville. In 1852 she was the youngest delegate to the Syracuse National Woman's Rights Convention, where she came to the attention of Mrs. Stanton. From then on, her association with Mrs. Stanton and with Susan B. Anthony was continuous and fruitful. With them, she was joint author of the three-volume *History of Woman Suffrage*, published 1881–1886. Over the years she addressed congressional committees and wrote several books.

In Matilda Joslyn Gage's own estimation, her most important work was writing *Woman, Church and State*, a 545-page book published in 1893.[13] This major work describes in graphic terms how the church, and the state abetted by the church, has demeaned women. Her understanding of the relationship between the church, politics, and power is remarkable as the following shows:

> As all churches seek influence in politics, we may rest assured that when the church as a whole, or any sect thereof, shall be found sustaining the political rights of woman or her religious equality in the church, it will be from the worldly wisdom of a desire to retain fleeting political power.[14]

Mrs. Gage recognized that the men of the church were only too ready to accept contributions of money and prayer from women, but could not abide their speaking in public. Apparently women had become bolder about requesting the privilege of speaking in churches to plead their numerous causes in the latter decades of the nineteenth century. (This may explain the overture from the Presbytery of Brooklyn to the General Assembly in 1872 quoted in Chapter 1). In the 1880's, according to Mrs. Gage, the Presbytery of Newark, upheld by the Synod of New Jersey, censured the Rev. Isaac See for permitting women to speak about temperance from the pulpit.[15]

May Women Speak?

By 1889 one Presbyterian minister, the Rev. George P. Hays, of Kansas City, Missouri, was intrepid enough to publish a Bible-study pamphlet entitled *May*

Women Speak? In this he attempted to demolish the arguments put forth by those who were opposed to women speaking because of the proscriptions of the apostle Paul in his letters to the Corinthians and to Timothy at Ephesus. Dr. Hays emphasized that Paul directed his admonitions to the church in two Greek cities, where the first women to hear the gospel would undoubtedly have been the Hetira, who served both as mistresses and as companions-in-public of the men. He claimed that it was these particular women whom Paul was cautioning the church about—not *all* women.[16]

But Dr. Hays did not stop with trying to refute the validity of Paul's admonitions about women. Rather, he went on to support not only women speaking in church but the ordination of women to the ministry as well. Citing a number of situations on the mission field, such as Muslim harems, where only women could go, Dr. Hays questioned the propriety of the Presbyterian Church's prohibition against women's administering the Sacraments.[17] He concluded his argument by asking why the Presbyterian Church could authorize presbyteries to make exceptions for uneducated men to be licensed and ordained but not for women. "God's blessing and success can make up for every other defect; but if a person's gender is wrong, no endorsement of the Holy Ghost and no favor of Christian people can atone for that in the eyes of the Presbyterian Church; nor indeed in any other evangelical church except the Quakers."[18]

In a Church Divided
the Women Move Forward

During much of the period when women were seeking the right to vote and to speak, the Presbyterian Church was struggling through a paroxysm of its own. The schism of 1837 left the church divided into Old School and New School Presbyterians. Like most schisms, the reasons for this one were complex. But three of the major issues causing the breach were missionary work, doctrine, and slavery.[19]

Eventually, in the South the Civil War brought the two factions together. But in the North, the breach was not healed until 1870.[20]

During these years Presbyterian women continued to form missionary societies and to carry on their benevolent work in spite of the divisions in the church.[21] Their societies were local in nature, and therefore not related to particular presbyteries or synods. As a result, they apparently were able to continue sending their contributions to whichever mission agency their own congregation supported.

Until the end of the Civil War, each local woman's society was practically autonomous, with the members determining their program and the objects of their giving. But the course of Presbyterian women's work began to change in 1867, when the wife of an Army colonel, Mrs. A. J. Alexander, wrote to her mother, Mrs. Throop-Martin, in Auburn, New York. Stationed with her husband in the territory of New Mexico, Mrs. Alexander vividly described the poverty, ignorance, and spiritual needs of the Mexicans, as well as the problems confronting the Rev. and Mrs. D. F. McFarland, who had been sent to Santa Fe by the mission board in 1866. Mrs. Throop-Martin shared her daughter's letters with the other members of her Female Bible Society. Moved to action, the women decided to organize themselves into the Santa Fe Association for the purpose of contributing to the missionary work there. Within a few months the association answered the plea of the Rev. Mr. McFarland for a teacher by sending Miss Charity Gaston of Ohio to help him with the school he had started.

Not content with this, Mrs. Throop-Martin enlisted the help of a friend, Mrs. James Graham, a member of the Women's Union Missionary Society of New York City. In 1868 Mrs. Throop-Martin visited New York City, where she and Mrs. Graham gathered a small group of women together and organized the New Mexico, Arizona, and Colorado Missionary Association.[22] The purpose of this new group was "to aid the Mission Board by contributing to the support of missionaries in these new territories and sending them Bible readers and teachers." [23] By 1870 the group had reorganized under the name, The Ladies' Board of Missions of the Presbyterian Church, and served as an auxiliary to both the Board of Domestic Missions and the Board of Foreign Missions. By this time, forty-two societies, half of which were in New York City and half scattered throughout the states of New York, Pennsylvania, and Ohio, had affiliated with this Ladies' Board of Missions.

Through the combined efforts of these societies the women in their first year had "paid the salary of a Bible reader and teacher in Santa Fe, assisted in defraying the expenses of a missionary in Arizona, and another in Colorado; aroused interest in behalf of the Pima and Navaho Indians, sent out Bibles, tracts, and three communion services."[24] Presbyterian women were no longer functioning simply as auxiliaries to the church's mission boards. They had embarked on a missionary enterprise of their own—a fact of major significance in the later history of women's role in the Presbyterian Church.

Five additional women's boards were founded between 1870 and 1888,[25] each with its own geographical focus, such as the Women's Presbyterian Board of Missions in the Northwest, and the Women's Presbyterian Board of Missions of the Southwest. Moreover, the domestic concerns of these various boards including work among Orientals and Indians, earlier considered to be "foreign missions," became part of the responsibility of the Woman's Board of Home Missions in 1878.

Just as the leaders of the women's rights movement learned that organization was the key to effectiveness, so too had Presbyterian women. This was the great achievement of women in nineteenth-century America. However, in the Presbyterian Church it took a man to show them how to make their potential count.

Presbyterian Women and
the "Bishop of the Rocky Mountains" [26]

No other man in the nineteenth century apparently had so profound a respect for or so deep an influence on Presbyterian women as Sheldon Jackson. Without his prodding and support, and without his opening up to women the channels to power, it is doubtful that they would have been able to create a power base as strong as they did—and as soon. Undoubtedly, he was motivated by concerns of his own, but that fact does not negate the reality of his assistance.

No missionary in the annals of Presbyterian home missions was so colorful or so controversial as Sheldon Jackson. Born into a religious family in Minaville, New York, in 1834, Jackson attended Union College in Schenectady and Princeton Theological Seminary. His goal was to become a foreign missionary. Rejected as not strong enough for overseas service, he was appointed as a teacher in a mission school for Choctaw Indians in Oklahoma.[27] There he contracted malaria, and after one year, moved to southeastern Minnesota to serve as a home missionary. Within a short time his "parish" covered thirteen thousand square miles. It was here that the pattern of Jackson's life and ministry was set. He sought to explore the religious needs and opportunities of the frontier, to establish churches wherever possible, and then to raise the money to support the work he had set up. This is where Presbyterian women came into his life—and he into theirs.

Jackson will probably be longest remembered for his work in Alaska.[28] In 1877, having previously been accepted by the Board of Home Missions as a regular missionary, he received a directive from Dr. Henry Kendall, head of that Board, to go into Montana and make a survey. Meanwhile, Jackson had received from a pastor-friend in Portland a letter written by an Army private to his commanding general, asking for help to set up a school for Indians in Alaska. While attending General Assembly in Chicago, Jackson tried to get someone to go in response to this call. Unable to do so, he ignored Kendall's directive, traveling on to Portland, where he found Mrs. D. F. McFarland (who had served with her husband in Santa Fe), now widowed and ready to explore the possibility of mission work in "Seward's Folly." The two of them set out for Alaska, where Jackson established Amanda McFarland at Wrangell, a primitive fishing village in southeastern Alaska. There she set up a school for Indian children.[29]

In the next six years Jackson managed to organize six Presbyterian missions with seven workers in the territory of Alaska. In addition he secured 17 teachers for the several schools which had an enrollment of over 500. Because of his prodigious work there and his knowledge of the area, Congress appointed him Commissioner of Education for Alaska in 1885.[30] Later, he is credited with having saved the Eskimos from starvation by introducing reindeer, a herd of which he personally escorted from Lapland.[31]

Jackson's determination to push on and to seize every opportunity for the expansion of missionary work created constant tension with the home missions agency in New York. In spite of their disapproval of his methods, however, the Board usually acquiesced eventually in granting him authorization to continue his enterprises. This was largely because Jackson was not only willing but able to raise the funds himself to finance his enterprises. It was probably out of this fund-raising experience that he came to see the need for and the viability of a Presbyterian women's organization whose major concern would be to support home missionary work.[32]

Jackson also needed allies for his mission strategy. His early contacts on the frontier had led him to seek out small groups of Christians, organize them into congregations, and then connect them with the Presbyterian denomination. To serve these congregations, he recruited seminary students or traveling preachers who used a settlement along the new transcontinental railroad as a base.

When he moved into New Mexico in 1870, he discovered that such an approach was ineffective, since there were virtually no groups of Protestant Christians to organize. The Mexicans in this area were about 80 percent illiterate; there were no public schools; the Roman Catholic priests had little contact with the people.[33] Jackson found that the people feared the Bible, since they were forbidden by their priests to own one. The Indians in New Mexico and Arizona had their own traditional religions, augmented by certain rituals, honoring Mary, Joseph, the Christchild, and the saints, that had been imported through the early Roman Catholic priests. Since ordinary preaching was useless, Jackson proposed that schools be set up to meet the people's need for education.[34] The Board of Home Missions, however, considered education outside of its field—not a valid part of evangelism. Also, there was no money for such a new approach to mission work.

So Jackson decided to voice his concern for the children of the Southwest by writing in the *Rocky Mountain Presbyterian*. He sought to persuade others of the importance of starting schools as well as churches. Women were particularly open to this idea and many groups responded as he had hoped.[35] In 1877 Dr. Kendall made an eloquent speech to the General Assembly in which he called for education to be recognized as part of mission work. As a result, the General Assembly authorized the synods "to appoint committees of women within their bounds to cooperate with the Board in the prosecution of this work."[36]

Thus began the long history of the relationship of Presbyterian women to the educational work of home missions, which connection lasted almost one hundred years. This action of the General Assembly also practically assured the formation of a national women's group to promote and support home missions—just as Jackson had hoped.

One biographer has called Jackson the "proposer and first advocate"[37] of a central organization of women to promote the work of home missions, similar to those already established in the interests of foreign missions. As early as 1873, Jackson promoted the idea of a woman's organization in his monthly paper, *Rocky Mountain Presbyterian*. This promotional bulletin, first published in 1872, was no doubt responsible in large measure for his success in raising funds. It was sent to all Presbyterian ministers, as well as to a long list of influential and affluent laymen and women. In it Jackson emphasized the need for giving to home mission projects, *not* in place of gifts to foreign missions but in addition to them. "Do not divide your gifts," wrote Jackson. "Give twice as much." [38] He also sent letters to a number of prominent women in the church, urging on them the formation of a united women's organization for home missions.[39]

In January of 1878 Jackson toured the East on a promotional trip. Everywhere he went he urged that a general convention of women be called for the purpose of establishing a women's organization. Even though there was widespread interest in the idea, no woman and no woman's group was prepared to take the initiative. So Jackson requested that the Board of Home Missions take steps to call such a convention. Since the executive staff on the Board was divided about the expediency of such a move, the Board refused. Then Jackson, in typical style, took the responsibility himself. Immediately he called for the women to come together in Pittsburgh on May 24, 1878, at which time General Assembly was to meet.[40] A number of prominent churchwomen gathered and showed strong interest in undertaking some kind of work for home missions. At the same time there was real opposition, stemming from a fear that such an organization might encroach on the responsibilities of the Ladies' Board of Missions in New York City. Rather than organize immediately, the group voted to appoint a committee to confer with the Ladies' Board about the "propriety of having their Board devoted exclusively to Home Missions." If the Ladies' Board refused to comply with this overture (which they did), the committee was empowered to call a meeting of women representing different churches from different parts of the country to form a new Board.[41]

During the next months, Dr. Jackson supported, encouraged, and assisted the women as they tried to decide how to proceed. Jackson wrote a letter to Mrs. Richard Haines of New Jersey, who was serving as corresponding secretary of the ad hoc committee (and who was also a vice-president of the Ladies' Board). In it he pointed out that the Board of Home Missions did not consider the Ladies' Board of Missions a national body but a regional one. He urged upon her the need for such a *national* organization so that women's groups not related to the Ladies' Board could participate more fully in home mission work.

When the Ladies' Board finally voted not to make home mission work the sole beneficiary of their efforts, the ad hoc committee appointed in Pittsburgh met on December 12, 1878, in New York City.[42] There they organized the Woman's Executive Committee of Home Missions.[43]

There is no reason to believe that Sheldon Jackson's primary concern was the promotion of women's rights in the church, or even that he had any great interest in the feminist movement as such. But his experiences on the frontier with female missionary teachers and with wives of missionaries apparently gave him an awareness of the courage and capacities of Presbyterian women. Then, too, he had frequently found that it was the women of the church who had been most responsive to his appeals for funds. Practical man that he was, Jackson must have realized that he and the work that he had initiated needed Presbyterian women, effectively organized, as his allies. The women had supported his drive to make education an integral part of the Board's work; they had supported him when he pushed on, unauthorized, into Alaska. As a kind of reward for this support, but probably more as insurance for the future of home missions, Sheldon Jackson was the prime mover in the effort to bring the national organization into being. As a consequence, Presbyterian women stood on the eve of a new development.

3

"THE WOMEN THAT PUBLISH THE TIDINGS ARE A GREAT HOST"

And what should be said of the host of Presbyterian women from coast to coast who have been the very fibre of this national organization? Hundreds of thousands of women who . . . have served as officers . . . or who as unofficered members have by gifts, by service and by prayer carried forward the cause. "The women that publish the tidings are a great host," and none but the Master Himself may follow the wide-diverging and far-reaching lines that through the years from generation to generation mark their service.[1]

M. Katharine Bennett

Once organized, the Woman's Executive Committee of Home Missions, whose major purpose was to promote the cause of missions in America, was not left to fend for itself. Sheldon Jackson, and to a lesser extent, Dr. Henry Kendall, executive secretary of the Board of Home Missions, continued to shepherd the new organization.

Dr. Jackson offered the women of the Executive Committee several columns of space in his monthly paper, *Rocky Mountain Presbyterian*. To promote their cause, the women wrote vivid accounts of the urgent need for more teachers on the home mission field. They made "mite boxes" available to local societies, and at Dr. Jackson's suggestion, they instituted a plan whereby women's groups could undertake the support of a particular missionary.[2]

Led by Mrs. Ashbel Green as president, Mrs. S. B. Scovel and Mrs. J. B. Dunn as vice-presidents, Mrs. R. E. Haines as corresponding secretary, Mrs. J. D. Bedle as recording secretary, and Mrs. M. E. Boyd as treasurer, the Executive Committee of the Woman's Board adopted a plan of operation. It promised (1) to undertake no work without the approval of the Board of Home Missions and (2) to strengthen women's work for Home Missions.

The goals and relationship which the women articulated indicate that the leaders in the Woman's Executive Committee were motivated more by a sense of responsibility for mission work in the homeland than they were by a search for power. Their intent was to serve, both the needs of people and the needs of missionaries, rather than to control. They fully recognized their dependence on the Board of Home Missions for approval of their projects and program, and they defined their goals in terms of responsibility for what they had themselves initiated. The goals of the women remained constant even though their relationship to the parent body changed, bringing the women to an unprecedented position of power.

The Woman's Executive Committee of Home Missions

In the first full year of operation, 1879–1880, the Woman's Executive Committee turned over $11,467 to the parent body and distributed boxes of clothing valued at more than $10,000 to the field.[3] Within five years they were contributing nearly $55,000 to the work of the Board of Home Missions. They had assumed responsibility for 86 schools with a total teaching staff of 175 among the Mormons, the Mexicans, the Indians, and the southern mountaineers.[4] Within five years, the mission work formerly conducted by such agencies as the Ladies' Board of Missions of New York and the Woman's Board of Missions of the Northwest and other regional boards was transferred by act of General Assembly in 1884 to the Woman's Executive Committee of Home Missions.

In this way the work of the Woman's Executive Committee rapidly expanded—by its own initiative and by transference from other agencies. In addition, the Board of Home Missions, which was having financial difficulties, asked the women to "assume all Home Mission work among the 'exceptional' peoples." [5]

Three factors probably account for the early success of the Woman's Executive Committee. The first was the women themselves. The president, Mrs. Green, was a woman of "rare ability and whole-hearted devotion." But the real force among the women seems to have been Mrs. Haines, the corresponding secretary. She worked practically full-time in the small storeroom offered to the Executive Committee by the Board for use as an office. There she wrote continually to the missionaries and to the supporting societies, giving both ideas and encouragement. As one Utah missionary wrote: "To many of us, the Woman's Executive Committee seemed to be personified in Mrs. Haines, and its energies and lively sympathies to be concentrated in her. She embodied its faith, its daring spirit, its conquering aggressiveness, and the largeness of its desire concerning the work which had been committed to it." [6]

The second factor was the establishment of a Woman's Committee for Home Missions in every synod (another of Sheldon Jackson's recommendations). With the Synod of Kentucky in 1885 completing the list of synods to appoint such committees,[7] the Woman's Executive Committee not only had broadened the base of its organization but it had a point of contact for its promotional efforts and a liaison with local societies.

In the following year, 1886, the Executive Committee began publishing its own magazine, *The Home Mission Monthly*, which became self-supporting within the next twelve months.[8] Soon after, the publication began to show a profit, all of which was turned over to the Executive Committee for its mission budget. The effectiveness of this magazine certainly contributed a third factor to the committee's success.

The practice of polygamy among the Mormons was a major concern of many Christian groups at this time. Punishable as a felony in the East, polygamy was practiced openly in the West. Mrs. Darwin James, who succeeded Mrs. Green as president of the Woman's Executive Committee in 1886, made a study of Mormonism and its concept of polygamy as a "divine institution." At this time, Utah had petitioned to become a state, and many Christians in the East were determined to block statehood until polygamy was outlawed there. Mrs. James carried the fight to Washington, where she had many contacts as the wife of a former congressman from New York. Over the years she visited four Presidents in the White House to plead this cause.[9] It was said of her, "Mrs. James could do more with the President in five minutes than could all the men combined."[10] In addition, members of the Executive Committee frequently went to Castle Garden in New York to talk with the single women who had been imported as a result of Mormon missionary endeavors in Europe. The women explained that, if these immigrants went on to Utah, they would become wives of polygamous husbands. On one occasion the women reported that they had been able to persuade "twenty Norwegian girls to return to their homes." [11]

Another issue of concern to the women of the Executive Committee was the plight of the Pima Indians in Arizona. They wrote the President of the United States asking him to appoint honest officials to replace the corrupt officers then in control of Indian affairs. From Congress they requested that a reservoir be built for irrigation purposes on the Pima reservation. One winter, with the Pimas facing starvation, they demanded that Congress appropriate money for food. In 1901, all Presbyterian churchwomen were asked by Mrs. James to write to Congress, asking for a full investigation of the conditions among the Pimas.[12]

While there is no record of their success with these ventures, the women of the Executive Committee did succeed in blocking the reinstatement of one of the men who had been responsible for a false arrest of Sheldon Jackson in Alaska. Jackson had become the champion of the Alaskan people in their fight against exploitation by certain white officials and traders. He had been arrested on false charges after he had embarked for the States. When word of his detention aboard ship—without the benefit of counsel—reached New York, arrangements were made for his release. The Executive Committee, along with the Board of Home Missions and the boards of several other denominations, petitioned the President for the immediate dismissal of all the responsible officials in Alaska, which was done. Sometime later, President Harrison received a letter from the "influential father of one of the offenders" asking that his son be reinstated. But the Executive Committee, under the leadership of Mrs. James, quickly sent a counterpetition to the President, and as a result, the reinstatement was not made.[13]

Certainly the record of the Woman's Executive Committee in its first decade of existence was remarkable. It was responsible for 100 schools and 274 teachers, "not counting those among the Negroes, which, though the Committee collected funds for them, were administered by the Board of Freedmen." [14] Even more remarkable, the receipts of the Executive Committee in 1889 and 1890 totaled more than those of the Board of Home Missions! The General Assembly in 1890 made note of this fact as follows:

> The Annual Report of the Woman's Executive Committee is the marvel of business clearness, but the success of their work is of chief interest. In 1889 the churches gave $266,395.20. In the same year the women gave $278,940.93. In 1890 the one gave $246,580.49 and the other $286,627.51, an excess on the part of the women of $40,047.02.[15]

During the next decade, the women's responsibilities continued to expand as they built a hospital in Sitka, Alaska, extended their work in the Southern Mountains, and established new day schools in California and New Mexico. The Board of Home Missions at this time asked the women to take over all the work in Alaska. The women demurred, indicating that they did not feel ready to assume such a task.[16] In 1890 the

Committee received a request from the First Presbyterian Church of Evanston, Illinois, seeking its help in working among the foreign-speaking peoples of Chicago, as well as other requests for assistance in the mining areas of Pennsylvania. The committee replied that it did not have the authority to initiate such programs and indicated that such work should be the responsibility of city missions. By 1895, however, the General Assembly had added "participation in the work in mining and industrial sections" to the committee's duties.

The story of the Woman's Executive Committee had its share of setbacks too. In the 1890's the women of the Executive Committee had to learn to cope with deficits. The "panic of '93" left them with a $37,000 deficit at the end of the year.[17] Administrative costs were drastically reduced, some day schools were closed, and attendance at boarding schools was limited. Mrs. James spent the month of August that year writing to wealthy friends seeking funds to apply to the deficit, but her efforts netted only $1,000.[18]

As the economy of the nation began to improve later in the 1890's, so did the receipts of both the Board of Home Missions and the Woman's Executive Committee. Even so, the General Assembly appointed a committee to investigate the financial records of these agencies, to determine the causes for continuing deficits. After the examiners had finished with the Executive Committee's records, they were apparently satisfied that there were no discrepancies. Miss S. F.

Lincoln, treasurer for the Woman's Committee at that time, reported that "manlike, in their generosity they suggested that the women help pay the debt of the Board." [19] Within the next two years the Executive Committee managed to eliminate their own debt and to assist the Board of Freedmen in overcoming theirs. Schools were reopened, and in Appalachia the women began supporting several pastors of churches that had been started as a result of the mission school program.[20]

There were other accomplishments, too, during these years. One was the establishment of a World Day of Prayer for Missions, initiated by the Woman's Executive Committee in 1887. This was the forerunner of the World Day of Prayer that today is celebrated by women in 168 countries under the direction of an International World Day of Prayer Committee.[21] A Young People's Department was set up in 1893 to promote home missions concerns among children and young people in local churches. Another accomplishment was the publishing of a prayer calendar "that societies might unitedly remember in prayer the missionaries of the Board on designated days." [22] The United Presbyterian Church still publishes annually such a yearbook of prayer.

During the last two decades of the nineteenth century a "great host" of Presbyterian women worked, planned, gave, and prayed. Their efficiency, their enthusiasm, and their effectiveness won the praise of the whole church, with the Board of Home Missions looking to them more and more for support and assistance. They were beginning to be a power to be recognized—*and* to be reckoned with.

A Committee Becomes a Board

In some quarters the Woman's Executive Committee was considered to be a local New York group, similar to the earlier Ladies' Board of Home and Foreign Missions. Recognizing this, the women decided in 1897 to change the name to Woman's Board of Home Missions. This change was in name only, for the new Woman's Board of Home Missions was still directly related to the Board of Home Missions and reported to it.[23]

The expansionist outlook of the women, so characteristic of the "booster" spirit of America in the nineteenth century,[24] continued as they moved into the twentieth. The end of the Spanish-American War provided the impetus for opening work in the Caribbean, first in Puerto Rico with two schools and a medical missionary.[25] Later on, they extended their program to Cuba and the Dominican Republic.

The new Woman's Board promoted its projects through its own magazine, *The Home Mission Monthly,* and through special leaflets and study materials prepared for both women's and youth groups in local churches. Women of other denominations were doing the same thing. Soon after the turn of the century, the women of several denominations issued an experimental study covering the work of each group.

As a result of this study, one of the first and longest lasting cooperative efforts was launched—the Missionary Education Movement—in 1902 at Silver Bay, New York.

In 1908, with the Presbyterian Woman's Board of Home Missions leading the way, an interdenominational group, known as the Council of Women for Home Missions, was established. That council became one of the parent groups forming what is now known as Church Women United, an independent movement of Protestant, Roman Catholic, and Orthodox women in the U.S.A. It was the Council of Women for Home Missions that set up a worker on Ellis Island in 1910 to aid the newly arrived immigrants, and ten years later began a ministry with migrant workers,[26] which continues today under the aegis of state councils of churches and other groups.

Perhaps one of the most significant events to occur in the Woman's Board during this time was the election in 1909 of Mrs. Fred S. Bennett of Englewood, New Jersey, to succeed Mrs. James as president. A woman of unique abilities, Katharine Bennett was to leave her mark, not only on the Woman's Board, which she guided through the rest of its life as a separate organization, but also on the status of women in the Presbyterian Church. After graduation from Elmira College, she had served for four years as Secretary for the Young People's Department of the Woman's Board before her marriage to Fred Bennett, a manufacturer. From her work as a board executive, and from her experiences as a member of the Woman's Board to which she had been elected in 1898, Mrs. Bennett knew the program and personnel of Presbyterian home missions as few did. According to those who worked with Mrs. Bennett over the years,[27] she combined a brilliant mind and the ability to write and speak effectively with personal charm and wit. Without her leadership, the story of the role of women in the Presbyterian Church would be quite different.

A Board Becomes a Corporation

In 1911 there was some question about the legality of the Woman's Board of Home Missions to receive legacies, since it was an unincorporated body. During that same year, the General Assembly suggested that the matter be investigated, so the Woman's Board appointed a committee. A report of this group was submitted to the Woman's Board in May 1912.

Until this time, in accord with the relationship outlined by the Woman's Executive Committee in 1879, the Woman's Board of Home Missions had been under the authority of the Board of Home Missions and accountable only to it. It was the Board of Home Missions, sometimes called The Assembly Board, that reported directly to General Assembly, including an account of the work of the Woman's Board. The prospect of the Woman's Board becoming incorporated as an independent body apparently posed a threat to leaders of the Board of Home Missions. The negotiations proved to be somewhat delicate.

The Minutes of the Woman's Board for June 2,

1914, indicate that Mrs. Bennett, the president, reported on the action taken by General Assembly in May in Chicago, namely, to refer the matter to the Executive Commission "with power to act after conferring with the Boards." [28] The matter was placed on the docket of the September 29th meeting of the Executive Commission of the General Assembly.[29]

Two weeks before, on September 15, the Board of Home Missions and the Woman's Board scheduled a joint conference to discuss the question. On that day a number of the representatives of the Board of Home Missions did not appear. The representatives of the two groups who were present agreed to request postponement of the question until the February meeting of the Executive Commission. In its Minutes for September 22, the Woman's Board reported that "the Boards will present a joint communication and that the Executive Commission be asked to withhold action on the subject at its meeting in Atlantic City on September 29." [30] This request had been an action of the joint meeting on September 15, and was duly reported to the Board of Home Missions on September 17, as well as to the Woman's Board.

After the meeting of the Board of Home Missions on the 17th, however, the clerk of the Board sent a notice to the Woman's Board that the Board of Home Missions had "voted that the incorporation of the Woman's Board at this time is not advisable." [31]

The response of Mrs. Bennett to this violation of the September 15th agreement was swift and sure. Meanwhile, she had received notice from the Stated Clerk of the General Assembly that the matter of incorporation was indeed to be on the agenda in Atlantic City on September 29, and that a special committee had been appointed with the Rev. Mr. Thompson of Minneapolis as chairman. Mrs. Bennett immediately notified the Rev. Mr. Thompson of her intention to be in Atlantic City on the 29th " in case the committee should desire information concerning the Woman's Board." [32] When Mrs. Bennett reported her action to the Executive Committee of the Woman's Board on September 22, that group voted support for their president's prompt action, and requested the vice-president to accompany Mrs. Bennett to Atlantic City, since it was clear that the action of the Board of Home Missions on the 17th was "not in line with the action of the conference above referred to," and therefore the Woman's Board was "at liberty to take action independently." [33]

Mrs. Bennett and the vice-president were not called before the committee in Atlantic City, but they interviewed many of its members. The Executive Commission of the General Assembly voted approval for the incorporation of the Woman's Board "but with such provision in the articles of incorporation as would make it auxiliary to the present Board of Home Missions." [34]

Several months later on March 2, 1915, Mrs. Bennett announced to the Woman's Board that the incorporation of their Board was accomplished, at least so far as action of the General Assembly and its Executive Commission were concerned.

As an adjunct of the Board of Home Missions, the Woman's Board had been subject to its control and jurisdiction. All property and all legacies were in the name of the Board of Home Missions, even though the programs related to schools, hospitals, and a growing number of community centers and even some churches, were financed and administered by the Woman's Board. The fact that the General Assembly decentralized the work of the Board of Home Missions, with some of its programs coming under the control of the presbyteries in which the projects were located, infers perhaps some dissatisfaction with the way home mission funds were being allocated. Since the Board of Home Missions was accountable directly to the General Assembly, it had no recourse but to accept its direction. This work of the Board of Home Missions was mainly concerned with the support of struggling churches. Therefore, it is highly improbable that presbyteries had much interest in taking on the added burden of administering the educational and medical work being done by the women. Since the Board of Home Missions held title to school and hospital properties and was the beneficiary of legacies designated for educational and medical work, the decentralization of the Board's work created a problem. To solve this problem, the General Assembly recommended that the Woman's Board be incorporated so that it could carry on the work it was already doing. Such an incorporation not only took control of the work of the Woman's Board away from the Board of Home Missions, but it also made the Woman's

Board responsible directly to the General Assembly, on the same basis as the Board of Home Missions.[35] It can readily be understood why the Board of Home Missions resisted this action, and why the incorporating charter of the Woman's Board made a point of declaring that its work would continue to be "auxiliary" to that of the Board of Home Missions.

At the next General Assembly, in May 1916, Mrs. Bennett as president of the Woman's Board, reported to the General Assembly, the first woman ever to speak in such a capacity from the Assembly platform. As one contemporary account states, "and talk she did—brightly, sprightly, and wittily, much to the point and entirely to the delight of the 900 men who made up her audience." [36]

In just one century Presbyterian women, with the help of men like Sheldon Jackson and Henry Kendall, had developed from a few widely scattered societies that sewed and saved pennies into a national agency charged with the responsibility of administering a program requiring hundreds of workers and hundreds of thousands of dollars each year. Their work was acknowledged by the whole church, as demonstrated in their recognition as an independent agency of the General Assembly. For the first time, women had achieved a power base in the Presbyterian Church.

Consolidation—and Co-optation

Under the leadership of Mrs. Bennett, the work of the Woman's Board of Home Missions flourished during the next six years. She understood the place of change in mission work, as well as the need for flexibility. The necessity for sloughing off the old to take on the new was a fact of church life that Katharine Bennett learned from experience.

But the exercise of power and independence that the Woman's Board enjoyed following its incorporation in 1915 was short-lived. By 1920 there was much discussion in the Presbyterian Church about the need to reorganize the boards and agencies. At that time there were thirteen such agencies. As a consequence, there appeared to be an overlapping of responsibilities and a missing of opportunities that frustrated church leaders. In 1921 the General Assembly appointed a Committee on the Reorganization and Consolidation of the Boards and Agencies to study the problem and to report recommendations the following year.

The meeting of the Woman's Board of Home Missions in January 1922 records the first of many minutes about reorganization and consolidation. The president had prepared a statement which was approved and sent to the Rev. John Timothy Stone, chairman of the Reorganization Committee.[37] In careful language it sets forth the consensus of the Woman's Board that, since it had been functioning autonomously for only six years, it deemed a change inadvisable. In part, the statement read as follows:

> The only wish of the Woman's Board of Home Missions in any plan of reorganization is
> (1) That the work that has been built up through many years shall be guarded.

(2) That the gifts which make this work possible shall not be lost to the Church.

(3) That the permanent funds, annuity gifts and field property that have been accumulated shall be conserved in accordance with the wishes of the many donors.

The Woman's Board of Home Missions having given careful thought to the method by which the above objects can best be attained, a majority of the members expressed themselves as feeling that a separate Woman's Board should be continued.[38]

The statement went on to point out that, if there were to be just one Board of Home Missions, it was questionable whether or not Presbyterian women would continue their "double giving," i.e., giving to home missions as individual church members and again through their missionary societies. In the estimation of the members of the Woman's Board, "the fundamental question . . . is the place and work of women's societies in the local church. If these have completed their special service they should be given up, but the Woman's Board is not prepared to say that this is the case." [39] The members of the Woman's Board could see the possibility of altering the focus of such local societies with an emphasis on "stimulating interest in missions," but they declared their conviction that local church societies that have no "direct financial responsibility tend to become lifeless agencies." [40]

Another point of anxiety for the women was the prospect that consolidation of the two home mission

Boards would place the administration of their schools and hospitals under the control of presbytery committees on home missions. The women feared that such committees might be too parochial in their outlook to administer institutions that served people from a wide area. Also, since the members of such committees were usually ministers, the women were afraid that their work would not have the benefit of being supervised by people trained in educational and medical fields.[41]

As a result of these concerns, the leaders of the Woman's Board took action to prepare and distribute to all commissioners to General Assembly in May 1922 a brief history of the Woman's Board of Home Missions.[42] They also sent five of their members to "take whatever measures seem necessary to present the attitude of this Board toward the Reorganization Plan." [43] Just as they had done seven years earlier in connection with the incorporation issue, the Woman's Board "lobby" was at work again!

By the fall of 1922, however, it was clear that some kind of reorganization would take place. At their September meeting, the Woman's Board voted to send a committee of three to meet with Dr. Stone's Committee on the Reorganization and Consolidation in Atlantic City in October. After that meeting, the members of the Woman's Board bowed to the inevitable—but not without a last concerted effort to ensure the continuity of "double giving" from women's societies.[44]

There is nothing in the Minutes of the Woman's

Board to explain their insistence on maintaining the practice of double giving. Their tenacity may have been due to an intuition that the only leverage left to them, after consolidation, would be financial. Couching this concern in terms of preserving among women's groups a sense of responsibility for home mission giving, the leaders of the Woman's Board persisted in demanding that women's groups be allowed to remit their monies directly through local and presbyterial society treasurers, designating it for educational and medical work as before.[45]

While the Woman's Board was unable to preserve its own independent existence, it did succeed in accomplishing its other objective. According to the Plan adopted by the General Assembly in 1923, a Division of Schools and Hospitals was created in the newly formed Board of National Missions. This division was given responsibility for all the educational and medical institutions administered by the agencies that were merged into the new Board of National Missions, except those "carried on by the former Board of Missions for Freedmen."[46] In addition, the Plan specified "that the Women's Missionary Societies of the local churches continue to specialize, as had been their custom, in the support of schools and hospitals now being carried on by any of the Boards, also of such special and otherwise unclassified pieces of work as have been initiated by and have been under the care and support of the Women's and Young People's Missionary organizations."[47] Thus both the integrity of the educational and medical work of the women and the system of double giving by women were preserved.

The Plan of Organization adopted in 1923 continued until 1972. Under it, the Board of National Missions became the largest and most complex agency of the denomination. In it were combined seven of the thirteen former agencies, and the change involved the "legal transfer of much property in many states." [48]

In addition to the Woman's Board of Home Missions, the new Board of National Missions took over the work previously done by the Board of Home Missions, the Board of Missions for Freedmen, the Board of Church Erection, the mission work of the Board of Publication and Sabbath School Work, the Committee on Evangelism, and the Committee on Army and Navy Chaplains.[49] The three other Boards created under the 1923 Plan were the Board of Foreign Missions, the Board of Christian Education, and the Board of Pensions.

According to Dr. Hermann N. Morse,[50] the "takeover" of the Woman's Board was no different from that of any of the other boards or agencies involved. It "was not in any sense an anti-feminist move," writes Dr. Morse.[51] While there is no evidence that the members of the Woman's Board regarded the reorganization as "anti-feminist," an article written by Mrs. Bennett in 1936 indicates that the change was certainly not accepted with unanimity. After commenting that each of the new Boards, with the exception of the Board of Pensions, was constituted with one third ministers, one third laymen, and one third women, she stated:

> For the future the women were not to serve in separate boards, but became an integral part of the general boards of the church. Here was change indeed. But *not* accepted unanimously by the women or by the church at large! Some felt it to be a backward step, some approved, and some would "wait and see." [52]

The last annual meeting of the Woman's Board of Home Missions took place on April 24, 1923. After reports were heard, "the meeting spontaneously resolved into a 'love feast,'" with "reminiscence of early days and early workers," as well as recognition of the officers of the Board, especially Mrs. Bennett. She was cited for "her executive ability, her beautiful spirit, and her fineness of leadership—a pilot who has steered the ship with no uncertainty." [53] A week later, on May 2, Mrs. Bennett was elected vice-president of the Board of National Missions at its first meeting, in which capacity she was destined to play another outstanding part in the developing role of women in the Presbyterian Church.

At the height of its power, the Woman's Board of Home Missions had promoted, financed, and administered a program of mission work extending from Alaska to the Caribbean with a budget of over a million dollars a year. The Woman's Board had met monthly, with a *weekly* meeting of the Executive Committee, to consider every detail of its program—

from the repair of heating plants in New Mexico to the building of a concrete fence in San Juan; from the appointment of teachers, janitors, and doctors to the awarding of a $300 scholarship to a mission school graduate so that he could attend Purdue University.[54] Since its incorporation in 1915, the Woman's Board had had complete authority over its funds, its personnel, and its program—accountable only to the General Assembly.

Even though the mission program continued much as before, and even though the same staff continued to administer the work, and even though the women continued to encourage Presbyterian women's societies to increase their giving, a change had occurred; an era had ended.

From our vantage point in history, there is little doubt that the demands of the time and the interests of the church were best served by consolidation. But the fact remains that, even though their mission work survived, and even though the practice of "women's giving" prevailed, the one power base developed by women in the Presbyterian Church—the Woman's Board of Home Missions—had been lost through the process of co-optation.

Certainly there is nothing to indicate that the *intent* of consolidation of the various boards and agencies was other than to eliminate overlapping programs, to streamline projects, and to manage resources efficiently. These goals the leaders of the Woman's Board understood and supported. Both boards were operating projects in some of the same areas, but there were discrepancies in style and in efficiency of administration. When the opportunity presented itself, the Board of Home Missions was fully prepared to merge with the Woman's Board, along with a number of less powerful agencies. By becoming the Board of National Missions, the new organization provided "participation" but managed "to maintain the decision-making power in its own hands." [55] In this way, formal co-optation was used to gain access to the power held by the women of the Woman's Board.

It is not known from the records exactly how the women felt in 1923 about what was happening to them. What is known is that they resisted the co-opting process at several points, but their resistance met with limited success. Too late they realized that their power had been co-opted. Too simply they thought that their loss of power was due to lack of equality in the church.

4

AFTERMATH AND THE DRIVE FOR EQUALITY

> With the purpose in mind of securing for women the same status in the Church as that now enjoyed by men, will it be wiser to seek such status as this for women at once . . . or will it be wiser to seek full status by degrees?[1]
>
> *Report of the Conference on the Status of Women, St. Paul, Minnesota, May 1929*

It was the Roaring '20s . . . postwar isolationism . . . Scott Fitzgerald and Zelda . . . Republican high tariffs . . . Ku Klux Klan . . . new morality . . . Warren Harding and Calvin Coolidge . . . flapper girls in short skirts and short hair . . . Al Capone and prohibition . . . women's suffrage won . . . prosperity and nationalism . . . fundamentalism versus modernism in the churches . . . change, change, and more change . . .

Described by some historians as "the decade of disillusionment," the '20s arrested the enthusiasm spawned by such "crusades" as the Student Volunteer Movement with its slogan of "Evangelizing the World in This Generation." [2] A new realism, a new sophistication took hold, with religion and the church no longer dominant in the lives of many Americans. According to church historians Smith, Handy, and Loetscher, "the tensions which the period had set deep within Protestantism erupted into the bitter fundamentalist-modernist controversy. . . . So this period of transition and turmoil . . . ended in a slump, revealing the toll of the years." [3]

The Presbyterian Church in the U.S.A. had already undergone a sweeping reorganization and consolidation of its boards and agencies. It had adapted itself to the new age, ready for the era of peace and prosperity that was promised. But it was to know no peace.

There was upheaval in the boards and agencies as offices were relocated and executives reassigned. There was turmoil among the clergy as they tried to separate heresy from orthodoxy. There was dissatisfaction in the churches as they sought to adjust to change. There was confusion among the women as they sought to understand their new responsibilities and relationships. This was a time of unrest as well as change—in the church as in society. So intense was this unrest in the Presbyterian Church that in 1925 the Moderator of the General Assembly took the floor himself to propose the appointment of a special commission to consider the "causes of unrest in the church." [4]

UNREST IN THE CHURCH

The tensions that surged and swelled into a full-scale storm centered around the group known as "the fundamentalists." [5] Found in nearly every major denomination, fundamentalism was nurtured in the soil of nineteenth-century millenarianism.[6] Ignoring the findings of historical criticism and seeing corroboration of their millennial views in the events of World War I,[7] the fundamentalists mounted an attack on liberalism in the postwar decade. That attack ultimately divided both the Presbyterian and the Baptist (Northern) denominations.[8] For Presbyterian fundamentalists, there were five particular points of doctrine around which the storm raged. These five points, first articulated in 1910,[9] included belief in "the inerrancy of the Scriptures, the virgin birth of Christ, his physical resurrection, his substitutionary atonement, and his miracles as changing the order of nature." [10]

In 1918 the fundamentalists called a convention in Philadelphia. There they mapped a strategy, which, according to one historian, was to "gain control of the organizations of the important denominations and form them on the Fundamentalist pattern." [11] The Northern Baptist Convention and the Presbyterian Church in the U.S.A. became prime targets in this strategy. Baptist polity, however, did not provide for any adequate means of prosecuting heresy, so the Presbyterian Church became the focal point of the struggle. Controversy centered on Harry Emerson Fosdick, a Baptist minister preaching in the pulpit of the First Presbyterian Church in New York City. Fosdick, one of the foremost spokesmen of liberal Protestantism, had been invited by the Session of First Church to be their preacher, even though he was not installed as pastor. By 1923 the power of the fundamentalist faction was sufficiently formidable in the Presbyterian Church that General Assembly, urged on by William Jennings Bryan,[12] brought judicial action against the Presbytery of New York for permitting such an irregularity. The attack on Fosdick was led by Dr. Clarence Macartney, the arch-conservative pastor of Arch Street Presbyterian Church in Philadelphia. It was a fight that continued in the ecclesiastical courts for two years.[13]

The denomination was deeply divided, not only over Fosdick, but also over the demand of the fundamentalists that all ministers and all executives of the new boards and agencies subscribe to the five points of doctrine. As a countermove, the liberals drew up a document in 1924 that set forth the historic freedom of interpretation permitted to Presbyterian ministers. Traditionally, pastors had always been allowed to interpret both the Scriptures and the Westminster Confession of Faith according to the dictates of conscience under the guidance of the Holy

Spirit. The document further declared that any action requiring subscription to other doctrines (such as the five points of the fundamentalists) was therefore unconstitutional.[14] Known as "The Auburn Affirmation" because copies of it were mailed from Auburn, New York, where Auburn Seminary was then situated, the document bore the signatures of nearly 1,300 ministers, or about one third of the total number in the church at that time. The General Assembly of that same year, even with Dr. Macartney as Moderator, upheld the point of view of the Auburn signers. That Assembly, however, again took action against the Presbytery of New York, requesting it either to require Fosdick to join the Presbyterian Church or to refrain from preaching at First Church.[15] Fosdick chose the latter course and soon became the first pastor of the new Riverside Church in New York City.

Even with Fosdick out of the way, the controversy continued to smolder. The fundamentalists selected two new targets in their fight to gain control of the denomination. This time it was Princeton Seminary and the Board of Foreign Missions. John Gresham Machen, professor of New Testament at Princeton Seminary, was the leading apologist of the fundamentalists.[16] After failing to purge the seminary of faculty members suspected of holding liberal views, Machen left Princeton in 1929 to establish his own seminary and an independent board of foreign missions. Because of such divisive activities, Machen, along with Carl McIntire and four other ministers, was deposed by the General Assembly in 1933. Soon thereafter, they set up a new denomination known as the Orthodox Presbyterian Church.[17]

The battle between orthodoxy and modernism was not, however, confined to the church in this period. In 1925 the Scopes "monkey trial" took place in Tennessee with William Jennings Bryan and Clarence Darrow as the protagonists. The issue in that trial went beyond the guilt or innocence of John Scopes, who was accused of having taught the theory of evolution in the public school in defiance of state law. The larger question concerned academic freedom. Is a teacher free to make use of the findings of modern science in public education or not? Basically this highlighted the same issue as the Machen controversy in the Presbyterian Church. In the latter case the question was, To what extent should Christians be open to the findings of modern historical criticism as applied to the Bible and theology?

One reason why these controversies were both decisive and divisive is probably that there was a strong countermovement working on the other side. This movement was composed of those who believed in progressive religious education, those who were involved in higher criticism of the Bible, and those who espoused the "social gospel."

In this era, a spirit of progressivism freshened old institutions. New discoveries in science and new ideas about morality challenged the old traditions. Change threatened, erupting in controversy, and leaving in its wake confusion, uncertainty, and unrest.

Unrest Among Women

Presbyterian women were not immune from the general unrest in the church. They were, however, more or less content to leave theological debate and ecclesiastical struggles to the men.

Of far greater concern to the women seem to have been decreasing revenues, especially for the Board of National Missions. By February 1, 1925, just 59 days before the end of the fiscal year (March 31), only 52 percent of the $1,344,000 budget allocated to women's and young people's groups for the support of the Board's educational and medical work had been received.[18]

Because of the decrease in giving and resentment on the part of some women's groups over the consolidation of the boards,[19] the General Council invited Mrs. M. Katharine Bennett and Miss Margaret Hodge[20] in the fall of 1926 to study "the causes of unrest among women." This assignment was part of the larger investigation of unrest in the church, referred to the General Council by the 1925 General Assembly.[21] At that time there were no women on the General Council, with only ministers and ruling elders eligible to serve. After the consolidation of the boards and agencies, however, the General Council invited the two women who had previously headed the women's boards, Mrs. Bennett of the Woman's Board of Home Missions and Miss Hodge of the Woman's Board of Foreign Missions, to become "corresponding members." They had a voice but no vote. To these women the Council committed the work of investigating the unrest among women in the church.

Before the consolidation a trend had become evident in local church women's groups toward combining the women's societies for foreign and home missions into one Missionary Society. As the numbers of united societies grew, pressure was brought on the women's mission boards for changes, such as a uniform fiscal year, cooperative promotional materials, and unified publications. As a consequence, the Woman's Board of Home Missions and the Woman's Board of Foreign Missions had met in 1916 and initiated action in the direction of unification. Meanwhile, the women in local churches went even farther in their work of consolidation by bringing into one association, or federation, their Ladies' Aid Societies (responsible for church suppers and other congregational "chores") and their missionary groups. Had the financial support for missions continued to increase, the trend toward consolidation of the women's groups would probably have been encouraged by the women of the mission boards. Instead, there had been a marked decline in support—which raised serious questions about the future of women's organizations in the church.

Because of their concern over the level of support and over the form of organization, the women members of the two mission boards, together with the women members of the Board of Christian Education, invited twenty-two women from the church-at-large to meet in New York City in May 1925. The purpose of the meeting was "to discuss the new relationships developing from the re-allocation of responsibilities by the Reorganization of the Boards in 1923, the relation thereto of the Women's Missionary Organization, and of the increasing number of inclusive women's organizations in the church, known as Associations and Federations." [22] The only visible effect of this conference was the creation of a three-board Women's Committee. But at least some of the problems and tensions facing the women of the church began to be aired.

About a year later, Mrs. Bennett and Miss Hodge launched their study of the causes of unrest among women by conducting a survey. Their work culminated in a 30-page report, entitled *Causes of Unrest Among Women of the Church*, which was presented by Mrs. Bennett to the General Council on November 30, 1927.

In their introduction, Mrs. Bennett and Miss Hodge quoted one prominent churchman who wrote in 1870: "Some of the most thoughtful minds are beginning to ask what is to become of this Woman's Movement in the church. Let it alone—all through her history like movements have started. Do not oppose these women and it will die out." [23] According to the authors, male opinion was about equally divided between that same attitude and "benevolent paternalism which felt it to be a pleasant thing for the women to organize and raise funds but which utterly failed to recognize a new force that had been unleashed." [24] The authors pointed out that the church *could* have begun a new era by creating a unified church in which sex differences would no longer be a factor—but that it had not. "It is not unjust to say that the masculine failure to recognize and to seize upon this opportunity has been the background of any present unrest." [25]

Citing the achievements of the women's organizations over the years, Mrs. Bennett and Miss Hodge pointed out that as women's knowledge of mission work in the church increased, so did their interest, and that stimulated their support—which amounted to $45 million given to the church by women's groups in the previous century! And then came the reorganization and consolidation of the boards, which the report commented on as follows:

> But when the church, by action taken by the men of the church with but the slightest consultation with the women, and then only as to methods, decided to absorb these agencies which had been built up by the women, the by-product of such decision was to open the whole question of the status of women in the church. Then women faced the fact that their sex constitute about *60% of the membership of the Presbyterian Church,* but that a woman as an individual has no status beyond a congregational meeting in her local church, and that the long developed and carefully erected agencies which she had cherished could be absorbed without a question seriously asked of her as to her wishes in this matter. The women looked about into business and professional life and saw women rapidly taking their place side by side with men, with full freedom to serve in any position for which they had the qualifications. They saw the church, which affirmed spiritual equality, lagging far behind in the practical expression of it; they saw democracy in civic

work, autocracy in church administrations. It should not surprise anyone that among thinking women there arose a serious question as to whether their place of service could longer be found in the church when a great organization which they had built could be autocratically destroyed by vote of male members of the church without there seeming to arise in the mind of the latter any question as to the justice, wisdom, or fairness of their actions. . . .[26]

The reorganization and consolidation of the church has been a thing that has made acute, if that be not too strong a word, the restlessness of Presbyterian women. The women have been praised, sometimes too baldly and too patronizingly, for the work that they have done and a rather frequent query raised the question as to why if they were able to do so well the work that they had carried, they should not have been consulted as to the proposed changes! [27]

In this way, the report established an unmistakable relationship between the co-optation of the women's power base and their demand for equality.

Another element of unrest highlighted in the report was the proclivity on the part of some sessions in local churches to "order" all organizations in the church to come under a "single budget." This meant that all monies raised by women's groups, instead of being sent to the presbyterial society treasurer for remittance to the boards for the support of those projects assigned to the women, were to be channeled through the local church treasurer. Some sessions and boards of trustees in local congregations had supplemented the church's deficit by appropriating the money raised by the women for their own causes.[28]

In concluding the report, Mrs. Bennett and Miss Hodge could hardly have been more direct:

> That woman is welcomed with graciousness to certain services in the church is granted, but to thoroughly understand any "causes of unrest," one must recognize that there are clear-cut inhibitions and that the woman of training and ability must work in the church if she desire, recognizing frankly that whatever her power to give service may be, there is a certain point of position and influence beyond which she may not go. . . . Does she want to preach? Not many of them do—as yet. Does she want to serve in the councils of the local and denominational bodies? Yes, many of them do. May she do so? Only in a few denominations, of which the Presbyterian Church in the U.S.A. is not one. . . .[29]
>
> What are the specific things which women wish in the church that they do not now have? . . . What they do wish is the removal of inhibitions which constantly remind them that they are not considered intellectually or spiritually equal to responsibilities within the church. Most ask for no one thing, only that artificial inhibitions that savor of another century having been removed, they may take their place wherever and however their abilities and the need of the church may call. Woman asks to be considered in the light of her ability and not of her sex.[30]

Through Mrs. Bennett and Miss Hodge, many Presbyterian women declared their dissatisfaction with their status and role in the church. The Bennett-Hodge report was a landmark in the long struggle of women to achieve ecclesiastical recognition, and it helped to pave the way for the eventual emergence of the professionally trained woman.

Pioneering in the Search for Equality

Earlier in the twentieth century, attempts had been made by individual women to be ordained as ministers. One of the first of these took place on April 15, 1912, when the Presbytery of Chemung in Central New York voted to "take Miss Rachel Gleason Brooks under its care as a student in theology." [31] The presbytery then voted "that since our church does not as yet receive women as candidates for the sacred office, the question of Miss Brooks' application be laid on the table for the present, and further, Presbytery overtures General Assembly for a definite deliverance upon the question of acceptance of women in general as candidates for the ministry and upon the case of Miss Brooks in particular." [32]

While this resolution was adopted by the presbytery, the overture to General Assembly was apparently not sent or not acted upon. The following year Miss Brooks appeared again, on April 21, requesting that she be taken under care of the presbytery. It is recorded that "after considerable debate Miss Brooks withdrew." The following morning the question of her candidacy was again brought to the floor, and finally approved by a vote of 11 to 10.[33] There is no further record about Miss Brooks in the Minutes of the Presbytery of Chemung.[34]

Five years later, this same presbytery became involved in another attempt to grant women some measure of ecclesiastical equality. The session of

North Church in Elmira, New York, had arranged with a member of that church, Mrs. Lillian Herrick Chapman, a spiritually mature and extraordinarily well qualified woman, to supply the pulpit while their pastor, the Rev. Herbert Harris, was in France serving as chaplain to the American Expeditionary Forces. In September 1918, an elder from that session appeared before the presbytery to make known the session's surprise in learning that "Mrs. Chapman had technically no right to occupy a Presbyterian pulpit," and to request permission from the presbytery for Mrs. Chapman to continue.[35] After extended debate, the presbytery voted to license Mrs. Chapman to preach within the bounds of that presbytery only. The motion was passed with one abstention and one negative vote, the latter being cast by the Rev. Robert C. Hallock of Dundee.

At the next meeting of the presbytery, in April 1919, the members were informed that Dr. Hallock had filed with the Synod of New York (the next higher judicatory) a formal complaint listing three counts: that licensing a woman was (1) irregular; (2) unconstitutional; (3) unscriptural. However, the Synod of New York had failed to meet in the fall of 1918 (one month after the presbytery's licensing action) because of the flu epidemic.[36] Dr. Hallock informed the presbytery that therefore he was appealing the case directly to the General Assembly, due to meet in May. After hearing the complaint in full, the presbytery voted to request that the commissioners who were to be elected as delegates to General Assembly be instructed to act as counsel on its behalf in defending the action of September 1918.[37] When the General Assembly met, the Judicial Commission ruled that the case was not in order since it had not been heard first by the Synod. Consequently, the case was referred back to the Synod of New York for action.[38]

The synod, meeting on October 22, 1919, appointed a judicial commission to hear the case. The following day the commission reported, pronouncing a judgment on the first point of the complaint only; i.e., that the licensing of Mrs. Chapman was irregular. The commission ordered the Presbytery of Chemung to withdraw the license and further reminded the presbytery that it should make use of the "orderly way of securing change in the Constitution of the Presbyterian Church"—by overture to General Assembly.[39] Yet, at that same meeting of synod an overture to General Assembly requesting permission to license and ordain women was voted down "in view of the fact that this matter has been referred by the General Assembly to a Committee to report to the next General Assembly." [40]

This statement referred to the action of the General Assembly six months earlier, in May 1919, when three presbyteries—Dallas, Columbia River, and Saginaw—had overtured the Assembly concerning women's status in the church. General Assembly had referred these overtures to the Standing Committee on Polity, which had returned both a majority and a minority report. The majority report recommended no action "since it radically alters the Constitution and has been brought to the attention of the Assembly by only three presbyteries."[41] Thirteen members of the Polity Committee had signed this report. The minority report, signed by seven members, including the chairman, S. Hall Young (who had been a missionary associate of Sheldon Jackson in Alaska), "recommended that the Assembly direct the Moderator to appoint a Commission, consisting of three ministers and two elders to take under consideration the whole matter of enlarging opportunities for women, and to report to the next Assembly."[42] The minority report was adopted by the Assembly, and a commission appointed with S. Hall Young as chairman.

As a consequence of this action by General Assembly, the Synod of New York declined to act in the case of Mrs. Chapman. The Presbytery of Chemung, however, took seriously the synod's admonition to seek change in an orderly fashion, and, on its own, overtured General Assembly to extend the privileges of official authority to women. This action was taken at the March 23, 1920, meeting of the presbytery, at which time Mrs. Chapman returned the license to the presbytery.[43] At its meeting in May 1920, General Assembly referred the overture from the Presbytery of Chemung to the Polity Committee, which recommended no action inasmuch as the subject was already in the hands of a commission of General Assembly.[44]

During that year, 1920, the Special Commission on the Official Relation of Women in the Church, headed by Dr. Young, had made a survey of over 100 ministers "prominent in the Presbyterian Church and representing various seminaries" plus 40 women who were "generally officers in missionary organizations or of wide reputation in other lines of work."[45] The commission built its study around three points: (1) What do the Scriptures say? (2) What is the practice in other denominations? (3) What are the results of the survey? Seeking guidance from both Old and New Testament seminary professors, the commission concluded that "the Scriptures do not forbid either women elders or women preachers."[46] The members discovered that nearly all other denominations admitted women to any position except the ministry. In the survey, more than half the ministers favored ordination of women as ruling elders, and more than half the women were in favor of ordaining women both as elders and as ministers.[47]

But after all its careful work, the commission reported to the General Assembly that it declined "to express an opinion upon the merits of this important question. It is divided in sentiment, a majority having expressed themselves as conservative. But it is united in the opinion that the question is of sufficient moment and has excited such wide-spread interest as to demand discussion and settlement by the Church at large."[48] The Commission then presented a resolution requesting the Stated Clerk to be directed "to prepare and send to the Presbyteries for their action the following Overture: Shall the Constitution of the Presbyterian Church in the U.S.A. be so amended as to admit properly qualified and elected women to ordination as Ruling Elders, with all the rights and duties pertaining to this office?"[49] This resolution was approved by the Assembly and the overture duly referred to the presbyteries.

The following year, 1921, the report on the vote from the presbyteries showed that 139 had voted in the affirmative, 125 in the negative, with 37 recording no action.[50] This meant that the overture was lost, since a *majority* of 152 (out of 302 presbyteries) was necessary.

Three years later, the Presbyterial of Cincinnati, along with several individual women, petitioned the General Assembly in a lengthy document that expressed open resentment about the destruction of the women's mission boards and about the structure of the new boards which were designed so that women would always be in a minority. The petition pointed out that the women gave over $3 million per year to the work of the church, work which was determined by General Assembly in which there were no women representatives. The women requested that General Assembly:

> 1) remove from Presbyterian rules and regulations the restrictions in connection with the participation of women in the affairs of the church, and
> 2) authorize them to organize a Women's Missionary Society of the Presbyterian Church in the U.S.A. which would have the power to a) appoint all women who sit on any of the General Assembly's boards, having equal rights with men; b) instruct these representatives; c) publish an official organ; d) receive all money from women's organizations designated for the work of the boards; and
> 3) disburse that money.[51]

The action of the General Assembly on this petition followed the pattern of other years—to refer the matter. This time it was referred to the General Council "with the specific request that the Council consider the petition during the ensuing year and report on the whole subject matter to the next General Assembly." [52] But the General Council, reporting the next year (1925), decided "that the petition could not be granted, and that the Chairman of the General Council should prepare a statement of the reasons for this action." [53] There is no record, however, that the chairman ever prepared such a statement.

The women in the Presbyterial of Cincinnati must have been busy during 1925–1926, for in that year they secured the endorsement of 25 other presbyterial and synodical societies for a second petition to General Assembly, presented in May 1926, which read as follows:

> Whereas: the restrictions in connection with the participation of women in industry, politics, and education have been removed, and
> Whereas: the reorganization of the Boards has materially changed the relation of the women of the Presbyterian Church to the work they maintained, and
> Whereas: the present policy of sex-limitation of opportunity and service is forcing Presbyterian women of ability into non-denominational lines of religious activity, and
> Whereas: the present policy of sex discrimination is depriving the Church of one of its greatest single assets, the leisure time of its educated women:
> We respectfully petition the General Assembly meeting

in Baltimore in May, 1926, to remove from Presbyterian rules and regulations the restrictions in connection with the participation of women in the affairs of the Church.[54]

Again the women were rebuffed. General Assembly refused to act on the petition, this time stating that "this matter was acted upon so recently by the Church that we deem the time is not ripe for another consideration of this important question." [55]

From 1919 to 1926 the road to equality and status for women in the Presbyterian Church had been cluttered with overtures and referrals, with petitions and rebuffs, with co-optation and resentment. Torn by dissension and theological controversy, the church had refused to take the cause of the women seriously—until Mrs. Bennett and Miss Hodge made their report to the General Council in November of 1927. Having initiated the study and report, the Council could not ignore its results. The church could no longer dodge the issue of the status of women. Righteously indignant over the disappearance of their power base, yet secure in the knowledge that their economic power was still intact, the women had declared their dissatisfaction and had demanded equality in the church.

Women in Other Denominations

The search for equality and status was not unique to Presbyterian Church women. The aftermath of the feminist movement affected other major denominations as well. In 1927 the Federal Council of the

Churches of Christ in America, in conjunction with the Council of Women for Home Missions, and the Federation of Women's Boards of Foreign Missions of North America, appointed a Joint Committee to make a study of "The Relative Place of Women in the Church in the United States."

The report of the Joint Committee dealt with only 22 of the 114 denominations surveyed, but the membership of those 22 constituted well over half the membership of the Protestant churches—25,111,032 out of 46,883,756.[56] The study was addressed to four main questions: (1) Have women full status as laymen in local churches? (2) Have women full status as laymen in the denominations, including participation in the highest legislative body? (3) Have they full status as ministers? (4) Are the women's denominational missionary societies conducted separately, or are they united with the general missionary boards of the churches?[57]

Of the 22 denominations, only 7 recognized women and men equally as clergy and laymen;[58] 14 did not ordain women at all; and one (the Methodist Episcopal Church) had, since 1920, accorded women partial ordination, which meant that they could be ordained as local preachers but were not admitted to the Annual Conference. (This latter privilege would have given them a guarantee of being assigned to a church.) Among the denominations that did ordain women to the ministry, the Congregationalists reported 78 women ministers in 1924, and 95 in 1926; the Disciples of Christ had between 125 and 150 ordained women, with the United Brethren estimating that there were 25 in their denomination. Among the 14 which did not ordain women were the Southern Baptists, the United Lutherans, several Methodist bodies, the Protestant Episcopal, and all the Reformed and Presbyterian churches.[59]

Regardless of the status permitted women in the various denominations, the General Findings from the Survey reported a certain commonality of experience and practice. Although women had full status in some denominations, as a rule, they did not fully avail themselves of it. The Findings continued:

> It is more difficult to obtain the psychology back of the actions—or lack of actions—which result in the limited status of women in such an institution as the church. It seems to be generally admitted that women frequently contribute the largest proportion of attendance at meetings, the majority of Sunday school teachers, the largest missionary intelligence and interest, the greatest spiritual power and loyalty, the largest devotion to personal needs, to visitation and philanthropy, the keenest value of team work and responsibility, the encouragement of the highest ideals, in addition to those duties once designated as "woman's church work" which consisted of furnishing flowers, serving food, raising funds by the "chore method" . . .[60]

In conclusion the Report recognized that men and women can make equal contribution, and stated

> that "the whole work of the church should be planned by men and women working together"; and that "changes

should be made if necessary for doing church work together as human beings. This must needs be a slow process."

Such tendencies as followed out may in time result in a church of men and women, for men and women, by men and women.[61]

Apparently dissatisfaction with their status in the church was not limited to Presbyterian women. Presbyterian women, however, could point to the interdenominational study to show that of the six major denominations which accorded women no standing at all ecclesiastically, five of them were either Presbyterian or Reformed; the sixth was the Protestant Episcopal Church. In all of the other sixteen denominations studied in detail, women were allowed some measure of representation in church councils even if they were not ordained as ministers.[62]

Presbyterian Women Persevere

As a direct result of the Bennett-Hodge report to the General Council, that body in February 1928 decided to hold a special conference as part of its November meeting. Fifteen representative women from various parts of the country were invited to share in the daylong meeting along with the members of the General Council "to consider the question of the place and work and relations of women in our Presbyterian Church." [63]

Meeting at Fourth Presbyterian Church in Chicago on November 22, 1928, they discussed five topics: (1)

The present status of women in the ecclesiastical organization of the church. (2) Women's organized work in the church, including such questions as: Are they satisfactory and effective? Are the women reached by them? How to strengthen and improve them? What is their present value and future scope, especially their financial responsibility and relation to the benevolence budget and the Every Member Canvass? (3) The relations of women of the church and of their organizations to women's organizations outside the church, both local and national. (4) Women's unorganized work in the church, including their share in personal evangelism, Sunday school teaching, influence in the home, in religious education in the home and vocational direction of life, especially in the ministry and Christian service. (5) "The underlying principles. What are the right ideals and principles of separate, cooperative or united work in the matter of the relationships of men and women; what are the distinctive functions and contributions of each; what lines of distinction would be preserved and what erased?" [64]

The Special Committee on the Status of Women, appointed to plan this conference, was continued by action of the General Council and requested to make a full report at the next meeting, scheduled for March 1929.[65] In that report the committee called for "a very careful re-study of the whole question of the teaching of the Scriptures with reference to the place and work of women in the Church." [66] The report went on to outline three alternative proposals for the consideration of the General Council: "(1) resubmission to the presbyteries of the substance of the overture presented in 1920–1921; (2) resubmission of the proposal to ordain women as elders; (3) removal from the Form of Government of any form of speech which is inconsistent with the recognition of the complete equality of men and women in the life and work of the church." [67]

The committee's recommendation to the General Council was to adopt the third most inclusive proposal, but indicated that if the Council considered this unwise, it would be satisfied with the second. The committee also requested that, if any matter was to be referred again to the presbyteries, the General Assembly suggest that "in determining the issue . . . the judgment of all the members of the churches" should be sought, so that the women could have a voice in the decision.[68] In addition, the committee asked that another conference be called, this time inviting one hundred women, including the women members of all the Boards, an equal number of women associated with women's organizations, and a like number of women unrelated to women's organized service in the church. It was proposed that this conference be held just prior to the meeting of the General Assembly in St. Paul, Minnesota, in May.

The Council received the report, authorized the St. Paul Conference, and voted 13 to 6 to accept the third proposal, which called for complete equality of men and women! [69]

At the May meeting of the General Council held just prior to the General Assembly, Dr. John Timothy

Stone of Chicago requested that the matter be reconsidered, because of its possible effect on negotiations for reunion with other Presbyterian bodies. A motion to postpone the action for one year lost by a vote of 19–2. Perhaps as a compromise, however, the Council did vote to amend their recommendation to General Assembly. Instead of the forthright third proposal approved in March, which would have sent the presbyteries an overture granting full equality to women, the Council voted to recommend that *three* overtures be sent down, so that presbyteries could have a choice.[70] Overture A was the original overture calling for full ordination of women as both elders and ministers. Overture B provided for the ordaining of women as ruling elders only, and Overture C would have permitted presbyteries to license women as "local evangelists" for one year.

There is no indication from the General Assembly Minutes that this section of the General Council's report engendered much debate on the floor. The recommendation was approved, and the three overtures were sent to the presbyteries.[71] Nor is there any indication that the suggestion of the Special Committee urging presbyteries to consult members of local churches, including women, was honored.

But if the male members of the General Council had any doubt about how women leaders felt on this issue, all they had to do was to read the report of the special Conference of 100 Women, which met on May 20–21, 1929, in St. Paul. While the conference's major agenda item related to women's organizations in the church, their Findings indicate a strong interest in the question of ecclesiastical status. The conference consensus was that the church could best be served by opening *all* forms of service without discrimination except ability and capacity. It voted to recommend to the General Assembly, then meeting in the same city, that the matter *not* be postponed for a year.[72]

Church publications during the following year carried a spate of articles about these overtures. The first of these was written, predictably, by Mrs. Bennett and Miss Hodge for the October 3, 1929 issue of *The Presbyterian Banner*.[73] In it, they urged the women of the church to "consider this matter, not from the standpoint of your personal inclination, but from the standpoint of the best service that women can render to the Church and from the viewpoint of the younger generation who will soon have to take on full responsibilities for the church service." [74]

By far the most eloquent of the opponents to the overtures was Dr. Clarence Macartney, a leader of the conservatives in the Fosdick case, a former Moderator of the General Assembly, and by 1929, pastor of the First Presbyterian Church in Pittsburgh. In an article published in the November 7, 1929, issue of *The Presbyterian*, Macartney based his objections to the overtures on lack of authority and on inexpediency, citing the "restlessness and craving for something new and different which has possessed so disastrously human society and human government. The demand for the ordination of women is but an ill-disguised form of that restlessness which, in the name of progress, would defy authority and found a new church and a new gospel." [75]

The following week *The Presbyterian* published a second attack on the overtures, this one written by Ethelbert Warfield, president of Wilson College for women in Chambersburg, Pennsylvania. Deriving his argument from the apostle Paul, Warfield addressed himself to a "practical consideration," i.e., the feminization of the church, declaring that the strength of the Presbyterian Church "has lain in a certain robustness which in its active aspect is essentially masculine." [76] He admits that many women possess "rare gifts of exposition and winning arts of speech," but "the power of the pulpit still lies in qualities which are masculine." For him, the authority of preaching "has long since come to be so associated with the form and person of a man that to men at least the pulpit ministration of women is incongruous, and to most women ineffective and provocative." [77] Thus the president of a Presbyterian women's college consigned women to their place!

Nevertheless, the Moderator of the General Assembly during this year, the Rev. Cleland B. McAfee, put his weight squarely behind the overtures. Writing in the January 16, 1930, issue of *The Presbyterian Banner*, he pointed out very simply that, first, no theological issue was involved—only a change in the Form of Government, not in the Confession of Faith, and, secondly, that "the proposals are purely permissive." [78]

In the December issue of *Presbyterian Magazine*, Mrs. Bennett gently reminded the church that it was not the women who initiated the overtures, but that they were the "logical result of circumstances." "It is unquestionable," she wrote, "that women would have contentedly continued their established service (i.e., through their Woman's Board) had the church itself not brought about changes. . . . May one say, courteously but quite frankly, that the unrest instigated by male voices in General Assembly, and that having already occurred, those same voters must now decide whether they are willing to work with women on a basis of equality, or, if not, what adjustments are to be made that will be mutually satisfactory." [79]

And so the arguments raged throughout the year. When the final tally was completed, Overtures A and C had been rejected by the presbyteries by a vote of 108 affirmative, 170 negative, and 7 not voting. Overture B permitting women to be elected as ruling elders passed by a vote of 158 to 118.[80]

One can only speculate as to what might have happened if the original overture opening ordination to women as both pastors and ruling elders had been sent down to the presbyteries, instead of the three separate overtures. It is entirely possible that it would have been rejected because of the strong feeling in the church against allowing women to serve as ministers. In that case, women would still have had no voice and no representation in the church. On the other hand, since there was also strong feeling that women should have some status in the ecclesiastical structures, it may have meant that the presbyteries absolved themselves of guilt by voting "yes" to the ordaining of women elders while preserving the *status quo* with regard to women ministers. The question remains—Was the impetus toward giving women full recognition in the church strong enough to have carried the original overture, or did the separation of the issue into three overtures simply delay the granting of full equality?

In either case, the fact remains that in the face of years of effort and argument, the women had won only the right to be ordained to a lay office. They could now have a voice and a vote in the decision-making bodies of the church, sessions, presbyteries, synods, and General Assembly. By the following year, 1931, five women elders were elected as commissioners to the General Assembly—one each from the Presbyteries of Los Angeles, Wooster (Ohio), Washington (Pa.), Southern Utah, and El Reno-Hobart (Okla.). The Minutes of the General Assembly record this historic occasion, noting that after the roll call, "At the request of the Moderator, Dr. Hugh Thomson Kerr, the five women, the first of their sex to sit as ruling elder commissioners in the Supreme Judicatory of the church, rose and were greeted by the Assembly." [81]

But the professional fraternity in the church was still closed to women.

PART TWO

Until 1930 the women's struggle had been fairly clear-cut. Women in the Presbyterian Church had organized for mission. Over the years they had developed an extensive program which they planned, financed, and administered. But in 1923 that program was co-opted into the new mission agencies of the church, leaving them token control, but without effective representation in the decision-making bodies. They reacted by working to rectify their lack of representation –and won the right to become elders.

Following their 1930 victory, the women leaders in the struggle for equality seemed to lose some impetus, retreating into those areas of concern in missions which had been their prov-

ince for so long. Meanwhile, another force had been growing in the church, the religious education movement. In the period between about 1925 and 1955, this was the one field open to women professionally in the church. Gradually, some of these women religious educators emerged to take up the struggle indirectly.

Their approach was less clear-cut, and more complex. They were fighting a kind of "two-front war." Religious educators, whether male or female, had generally been viewed with condescension by the ordained clergy. Therefore, many women religious educators were more ardent in their pursuit of acceptability as professionals than they were in their fight for equality as women. Ultimately, it was this bifocal vision that caused the women in the religious education movement to lose the power that they once attained. Wanting to prove their competence and to validate their field of service, the women religious educators eagerly co-opted men into that field. In contrast to the experience of 1923, it was women who used the co-optation process. But, in so doing, they permitted the cause to get out of control, and consequently once again, the women lost their power.

It is not within the purview of this book to trace the history of the religious education movement. However, to understand what took place among the women involved in that movement, a brief sketch is in order. In addition, it is important to examine the move toward ordination of women as ministers that culminated in 1956, and describe the aftermath of the struggle for equality in the situation of women in the Presbyterian Church in the decade of the '60s.

5

"BOTH MEN AND WOMEN MAY BE CALLED TO THIS OFFICE"[1]

The ordination of women to be ministers was simply an idea whose time had come.[2]
Hermann N. Morse

The only indication of how the women of the Presbyterian Church reacted to the crucial, long-awaited vote on ordination in 1930 comes from an article in *Women and Missions*. It reported on the General Assembly meeting as follows:

> One of the Cincinnati papers made the statement that the 142nd General Assembly of the Presbyterian Church of the USA had opened uneventfully without any great issue—meaning controversial issue. The report on the status of women proved that the Assembly as a whole accepted the result of the year's voting with very

perfunctory interest. That the vote to allow women the right to occupy the pulpit in the capacity of ministers was lost by 171 votes to 106 votes hardly occasioned a murmur, and the victory of the second part of the overture, which gives women the right of being elected as elders, was received with only feeble applause.[3]

The inference from such a comment might be that the women were disappointed, frustrated, and tired. The lack of any further comments on the subject in subsequent issues of their magazine and the enthusiasm with which they delved into the promotion of what was left of their missionary enterprise would indicate that this was indeed the case.

In the meantime, during the '30s another group of women began to emerge seeking status for themselves. This group grew out of the religious education movement which had been something of a "stepchild" of the church since its inception in the early '20s.

The Rise of the Religious Education Movement

The Sunday school movement of the nineteenth century spawned the religious education movement of the twentieth. Originally it was a lay movement, emphasizing knowledge of the Bible as the way to salvation. Armed with songs and stories, "Bible men and women" followed the wagon trains westward.[4] Often they were the first and sometimes the only contact that people on the frontier had with religion.

These Bible teachers, who were supported by funds from the East, especially by women's missionary groups, brought hope for the afterlife to a people preoccupied with death, which was a constant companion in that time.[5] The Sunday school movement, nurtured by zeal from the Religious Awakening of the mid-1800's, flourished on the frontier. When missionaries arrived to establish churches on the frontier they frequently found that the Sunday school was already there.[6] This gave rise to a kind of parallel existence between the church and the Sunday school. As the church became more firmly established, the Sunday school continued. The Sunday school met in the church building on Sunday morning, but frequently involved an almost entirely different group of people. In general, the church was run by the minister and a few men of the congregation, with the Sunday school in the hands of the lay people, mostly women. This meant that the Sunday school was often considered as a kind of "stepchild" by the church.

The Sunday school, however, was a powerful force in the molding of religious concepts and moral values among American Protestants.[7] The faith that was taught was a simple faith in the rewards of being "good"—to be assured of a home in heaven after death.[8] Generally speaking, the path to heaven was by way of conversion, of repentance of one's sins, and of faithful attention to one's piety by reading the Bible and praying. Somehow these images and ideas took hold of the American psyche in a way that the more sophisticated teachings of the clergy about the paradox of Christianity and the offense of the gospel seemingly never did. As a result, there is a kind of parallelism that persists even today between the church and Christian education.

As the new era of the 1900's dawned, with adolescence emerging as a separate stage of life, with the rise of industrialization, and with new values challenging Victorian practices, the old Sunday school began to show signs of obsolescence.[9] John Dewey and his followers were developing new educational methods based on the perceived needs of children. At the same time, Biblical scholars were raising questions about the authenticity of certain portions of the Scriptures. Walter Rauschenbusch and others were proclaiming a "social gospel" in which they declared that not only must the individual be converted but the structures of society must be radically altered also.[10]

All of this inevitably had its effect on the church, particularly on the church's educational program. Some leaders in the church began to be embarrassed by the ineptness and ineffectiveness of the Sunday school, and they demanded reform.[11] To further this reform, the Religious Education Association was established in 1903 under the leadership of William Rainey Harper, president of the University of Chicago.[12] This association provided a focal point as well as a force for reform that soon permeated denominational boards of education. The International Council of Religious Education, organized in 1922, set about the task of bringing the latest findings in the field of education to bear on curriculum planning and production and on teacher training.[13]

These reforms brought into being a new breed of church educator—the professional. For the most part, they were not recognized as professional educators by those in the public education field, nor were they welcomed by the lay leaders in the Sunday school movement who sometimes felt they were being patronized.[14] Even so, a new field had been opened, a field open to women, who were considered by the culture to be peculiarly well equipped to deal with children and young people. As a result, many denominations, including the Presbyterians, began to experiment with professional training in religious education.

Presbyterian Training Schools

The first Presbyterian school established for this purpose was the Philadelphia School for Christian Workers, founded in 1907 jointly with the Reformed Church in America.[15] Both men and women were enrolled, but there was housing for women only. For a number of years the school offered several kinds of training—a three-year course for deaconesses and directors of religious education, a two-year course for pastor's assistants, and a one-year course for church secretaries. By 1928 the Bachelor of Religious Education (B.R.E.) degree, requiring four years, was available, and three years later only that course, providing complete college and vocational training, was offered. In addition, the name of the school was changed to Tennent College of Christian Education.[16]

The Presbyterian Church in the U.S.A. founded a second religious training school, in 1908, this time in the Midwest, the Presbyterian College of Christian Education. Located in Chicago, it later merged with nearby McCormick Theological Seminary, just as Tennent College merged with Princeton Seminary in 1944. Until 1915 only women students were enrolled, but later men were permitted to register to be trained "for Christian and philanthropic work." [17] Between 1910 and 1928, there were 300 graduates.[18]

Here was the parallel pattern at work again. The seminaries were training men to be pastors of churches, and the religious education schools preparing women for Christian education, i.e., Sunday school work. The men were being prepared to preach by learning Greek, Hebrew, homiletics, and Biblical exegesis. The women were being trained to teach by learning methodology and child development. For the men, the training was on the graduate level; for the women, it was undergraduate training.

In central New York, Auburn Seminary took a somewhat different approach. In 1921 the seminary itself opened a School of Religious Education "to meet the growing need in the Church for men and women adequately prepared for leadership and work as laymen . . . and to put by the side of the pastor well-trained men and women who will be his intelligent and sympathetic helpers in his work." [19] This school was on a *graduate* level, requiring a baccalaureate degree for entrance. The two-year course included Bible courses, church history and doctrine, as well as five hours of field work per week. At the end of the course, the student received a special certificate. In addition, Auburn Seminary offered a special short course (five-week) for the training of volunteer workers such as Sunday school teachers, superintendents, etc.[20]

In the years that the School of Religious Education functioned at Auburn (1921–1939) the student body was largely composed of women. In 1948, of the 205 alumni living, 178 were women, only three of whom were wives of male students in the Auburn School of Religious Education.[21]

Unfortunately, just as the religious education movement began to take hold in American churches, the Depression came. Because the position of professional director of religious education was so new, in many instances churches faced with declining budgets eliminated this staff position. The number of professionally trained religious educators, however, at this time was relatively small. Since most of them were single women and therefore paid less than married men, many of the women did not feel the job squeeze. Correspondence with several graduates of religious education schools in the '30s documents this experience. For example, one male religious educator, a graduate of the Boston University School of Religious Education in 1931, could not secure a church position immediately,[22] even though several women seeking jobs at that time had a variety of positions open to them.[23]

While the salary factor was probably of primary importance in the Depression years, it must be remembered that cultural attitudes concerning the proper spheres of activity for men and women also played a part. Religious education was considered a proper field for women, in much the same way that public school teaching was. In fact, several women who became religious educators did so after experience in public education, thus combining their interest in children with their commitment to the church.[24] This factor tended to freeze the pattern of parallelism between the church and the religious education field noted above.

Although all the religious educators surveyed by the writer indicated deep appreciation for the satisfactions that they derived from their work, there was a recurring note of resentment apparently based on the feeling that their work was neither sufficiently recognized nor properly paid.

Search for Status

As the Depression wore on, it became apparent to those in the field that religious education—relegated to women, underpaid, with no voice or vote in ecclesiastical circles—was of secondary significance in the church. Those who had entered this new field with conviction and enthusiasm found themselves, on the one hand, suspect by the clergy who felt superior in training and outlook, and on the other hand, suspect by lay leaders of the Sunday school program. Things had gone well enough until the professionals began meddling in curriculum and teacher training. With no standing in presbyteries, many of the religious educators found themselves watching from the sidelines as decisions "affecting church schools, youth work, etc. were being made . . . [by] unqualified clergy." [25]

So it was that the impetus grew for achieving some kind of recognition and status for religious education. Denominational leaders in the field, many of whom were men, enlisted the support of religious educators across the church, most of whom were women, for this purpose. In 1937, the Presbytery of Chicago overtured the General Assembly "to direct the General Council in conference with the Bd. of Christian Education to prepare standards for the admission of such lay workers to a classification to be known as 'Commissioned Lay Workers.'" [26] This was done, and the recommendation of the General Council to the General Assembly was approved in May of the following year establishing the "status of Commissioned Church Worker."

There is no record of any debate or opposition to this action, either in the General Council or the General Assembly, perhaps because the action did little more than set up standards and a certification procedure for religious educators. Included in the standards were the following: (1) membership in the Presbyterian Church U.S.A.; (2) graduation from high school, plus at least four years of study in approved schools, two years of which were to be specific training for church workers (no degree required); (3) personal appearance before the presbytery and annual examination while under care of the presbytery; (4) affirmative answer to five questions asked by the moderator of the presbytery prior to commissioning. The names of all commissioned church workers were to be listed annually in the General Assembly Minutes; the commissioned church worker's name could be transferred from one presbytery to another upon request and approval.[27]

By this action, General Assembly opened the way for a presbytery to exercise some control over the training of religious educators within its bounds. The religious educator, however, gained little but a title and passing recognition—no vote and no voice in presbytery meetings, no involvement in presbytery committees, no guidelines for salaries, no pension, and no recourse for judgment.

As an effort to raise the status of the religious educator in the life of the Presbyterian Church, the 1938 action establishing the status of commissioned church workers could be considered a failure. However, the action did accomplish a long-sought goal: for the first time in its long history, the Presbyterian Church had established standards and procedure for certifying a professional ecclesiastical office open to women. The professionally trained woman had come into being in the Presbyterian Church at last!

Aftermath of Recognition for Religious Educators

With the aid of a number of male religious educators, who were interested mainly in upgrading the status of Christian education in the church, women had finally gained a toehold on the path toward ecclesiastical status and equality. Like the men, however, the women involved in seeking status were more concerned about gaining representation on decision-making bodies as religious educators than as women. There is no evidence of any real self-conscious desire to achieve ecclesiastical recognition for themselves as women; rather, they wanted to bring religious education into the mainstream of the church's life and program.

This very lack of self-consciousness on the part of women religious educators may account for what happened subsequently. In fact they did not recognize what they had achieved as women. As a result they lost it—as will be shown in Chapter 6.

The Saga of Commissioned Church Workers

The first year that commissioned church workers were listed in the General Assembly Minutes (1939) shows that 9 presbyteries had commissioned a total of 15 persons: 13 women and 2 men. By the end of World War II, there were 99, 10 of whom were men. A decade later, the Minutes list 237 commissioned church workers, only 16 of whom were men.[28]

But these statistics do not tell the story of what really happened. After the 1938 action by the General Assembly, many directors of religious education who had been working for a number of years took advantage of the new status; many did not. For example, out of 8 Christian education specialists surveyed, all of whom are now retired, only 3 (2 women and 1 man) became commissioned. The others indicated that they had seen no need for this new status for themselves. Of the 3 who were commissioned, only the man felt that commissioning had been advantageous.[29]

During this period the nation was in the throes of moving out of the Depression into the all-out military effort of World War II. Institutions, as well as individuals, were caught up in changing priorities and programs. Within the church, ministers were turning to chaplaincy service, so that there was a shortage of trained personnel. With military bases mushrooming across the nation, women were recruited for service in housing areas surrounding these bases to minister to families of servicemen. Denominational foundations, such as the Westminster Foundation in the Presbyterian Church, hired women in increasing numbers for student work on college and university campuses. Local churches turned to professionally trained women to assist in keeping their programs going.

In answer to the growing need for trained personnel in the church, General Assembly appointed a Special Committee on Theological Education in 1942. As part of its findings reported the next year, this committee included a request that the Board of Christian Education "restudy the act establishing the status of Commissioned Church Worker," [30] recommending that the Board also consider the possibility of submitting the matter to the presbyteries "in proper form in order that it may become a part of the Constitution of the church." [31]

Thus began a study that lasted five years. Each year a "progress report" was made to General Assembly, citing difficulties and complexities and requesting a year's extension. Finally, in 1948 the Board of Christian Education recommended to the General Assembly that an overture be submitted to the presbyteries for action. In introducing this overture, the report of the special committee explained that, "after careful study, the Board is convinced of the inadequacy of the 1938 Act of the General Assembly establishing the status of commissioned church worker."[32] This overture, recommending that the inadequacies be corrected, was approved by General Assembly in 1949.[33]

As a result of this action, commissioned church workers made two major gains: (1) the standard for commissioning was raised so that only those who had completed two years of specialized training in an accredited seminary, or who had a master's degree (or its equivalent) were eligible, and (2) the presbytery was required to approve the invitation of a local congregation to a commissioned church worker and to install that person. For the commissioned church worker this meant that the educational standard set was *nearly* on a par with that for ordained clergy (i.e., two years of seminary training resulting in a master's degree compared with three years and a B.D. degree). In addition, the action meant that the presbytery was involved with the commissioned church worker and the local congregation in both the invitation and the installation, as well as in the dissolution process. As a result, the unordained person was no longer subject to the whim or prejudice of a particular pastor or session, but had some measure of "job security."

Intramural Tensions

At this point in time, it is perhaps impossible to understand fully the complexities that necessitated such a long period of study before revising the commissioning procedure. But it is apparent that tensions existed within the religious education movement, particularly between professionally trained directors of Christian education, most of whom were women with a master's degree (or equivalent) from an accredited seminary, and those women with a bachelor's degree in religious education.[34] Many with B.R.E. degrees were graduates of Presbyterian colleges supported in part by the Board of Christian Education. These tensions created a dilemma for the Board. It had to face the question of whether or not to recommend upgrading the certification requirements for commissioned church workers at the risk of leaving graduates of its own related colleges with no way to achieve ecclesiastical recognition.

Then, too, tension between the seminary-trained women and the ordained clergy added another dimension to the problem. Was it the third year of seminary training and a Bachelor of Divinity degree that entitled one to pension benefits? Or was it the act of ordination? With ordination closed to women at the time—whether they held a B.D. degree or not—how could women, working full time for the church, qualify for pension benefits? Without pensions, and with generally lower salaries, how could women responsibly afford to work for the church? Was it perhaps the Board of Pensions that wanted to limit its liability by excluding the commissioned church workers from its plan?

According to Dr. Ray J. Harmelink, associate general secretary of the Board of Christian Education from 1956 to 1966, and deeply involved in the revision of the commissioned church worker status, the tensions described above had always existed.[35] Because of the scarcity of professionally trained directors of Christian education during the post-World War II years, however, these tensions were accentuated.

Demands and Pressures

The 1940's saw the birth of several national denominational organizations that had implications in the field of Christian education. Particularly significant was Westminster Fellowship for junior high and senior high youth—organized in local churches, presbyteries, synods, and nationally, which was formed officially in 1942. This youth program, along with Geneva Fellowship for young adults, required adjustments in attitude and made new demands on leadership on the part of Christian educators.[36] At the same time, the Presbyterian Women's Organization was authorized in 1942, and the Presbyterian Men's Organization in 1948. During these same years the Presbyterian Church was creating a new church school curriculum, which emphasized the partnership of home and church in Christian education. Materials were prepared for parents' use as well as teaching plans for Sunday sessions.

The church was a "going" concern. Jobs were plentiful. Church budgets, both locally and nationally, increased annually. There was an atmosphere of enthusiasm and euphoria in the Presbyterian Church during this time.[37] There was also a deep concern on the part of some church leaders, especially those involved in personnel services, that the Presbyterian Church must find ways to recruit "able, qualified, dynamic young people into church occupations in sufficient numbers to keep pace with and to foster the denomination's growth." [38]

By 1947 the demand for directors of Christian education was such that "for every professionally prepared person with a master's degree in that field, there were at least two dozen vacancies reported, and the positions remained unfilled." [39] Denominational leaders looked at the statistics and began to be apprehensive about the church's ability to produce qualified professionals in adequate numbers. Admittedly, there was a shortage of Christian educators. But, in addition, during the years of World War II, the number of potential ordained clergymen graduating from seminary steadily declined to the point that there were fewer men entering the ministry each year than were leaving because of retirement or death.

As a consequence, the Presbyterian Church in the U.S.A. in 1944–1945 mounted an intensive recruiting campaign, which continued for the next five years. Four "Traveling Fellows"—two women college graduates and two men seminary graduates—were enlisted each year for a one-year "fellowship." The "TFs" (as they were called)[40] visited colleges and universities, local churches, presbytery and synod youth rallies, summer conferences and camps to present the claims of "church vocations," including the ministry, mission work, religious education, church social work, and the like. Interviews with interested youth were followed up by the Office of Vocation in the Board of Christian Education with a letter acknowledging their interest and offering guidance as requested. Young people interested in mission work were referred to the mission boards. In addition, a national organization for young people seriously considering church vocations was established under the name Celtic Cross. Presbyteries were encouraged to invite Celtic Cross members within their bounds to meet each January for support, discussion, and worship.

The Traveling Fellows were equipped with an Enlistment Kit full of a variety of pamphlets for distribution. At the conclusion of each interview with an interested individual, the Fellows were instructed to select the appropriate leaflet to leave with the interviewee. Included in the kit was one pamphlet entitled *Nine Questions About the Ministry*, which bore the silhouette of a boy's head on the front. Occasionally girls would ask about entering the ministry. The Traveling Fellows were given no particular directions about how to handle this question if asked by a girl,[41] other than the obvious one of directing her attention to the field of Christian education.

Of Commissioning and Certifying

During the post-World War II era with its focus on new church development and recruiting, the tensions among church educators had continued unresolved. In 1948 another national organization came into being, the National Association of Directors of Christian Education (NADCE). This association included in its membership both seminary-trained women and those with undergraduate training only, as well as a few ordained men. Anyone who was professionally *employed* in the field of Christian education was eligible. Each year at their meeting (which usually preceded by one day the annual conference sponsored by the International Council of Religious Education), there were conversations and programs dealing with the role and status of the Christian educator in the Presbyterian Church.[42]

In spite of all the study and revisions related to the status of commissioned church worker the problems were far from settled. So in 1952, the General Assembly was again overtured for "clarification of matters related to Commissioned Church Workers." [43] The overture was presented in the form of five questions concerning such issues as whether or not the presbytery was required to hold an installation service for a commissioned church worker, whether or not the presbytery's examination in theology should be as rigorous in the case of a candidate for commissioning as for ministerial candidates, and under what circumstances commissioning should be given and retained.[44] Once again the matter was referred to a committee, which reported to the 1953 General Assembly that it was making "progress." [45] In 1954, the report to General Assembly requested that an overture be submitted to the presbyteries to change the Form of Government to incorporate clarification of these questions.[46] By a vote of 242 affirmative to 3 negative, the presbyteries approved the proposed changes in 1955.[47] These changes mandated installation for the commissioned church worker if employed by a local church, limited the "commission" to work within the denomination, and declared the presbyteries to be "judge as to the sufficiency of the examination." [48]

Another point at issue among church educators was the difference in status between the commissioned church workers (those with graduate degrees) and those with only undergraduate training. As a consequence of this debate, an overture was presented to the General Assembly in 1958 proposing the creation of yet another status—that of certified church educator. This proposal recognized the right of presbyteries to grant "a certificate valid for a period of three years . . . to a man or woman who shows evidence of having received a bachelor's degree from an accredited Presbyterian college which offers an approved program of preparation for service in Christian education, or the academic equivalent thereof." [49] This certificate is renewable from year to year provided the educator "is pursuing a course of advanced studies, satisfactory to the presbytery, leading to the office of commissioned church worker in education or ordained minister." [50] This overture was approved, and in 1960 the office of certified church educator was added to the Form of Government.[51]

By this action, General Assembly gave standing to those who held bachelor's degrees in religious education and who were working in local churches as assistants in Christian education. Thus the dilemma of the Board of Christian Education was resolved by recognizing the graduates of its colleges as now having status. But the addition of certification to the roster of ecclesiastical offices, including commissioning and ordination, hardly solved the problem. Rather, the problem was merely postponed until 1963, when an overture that would have permitted commissioned church workers to vote in presbytery was presented and referred to the Special Committee on the Nature of the Ministry,[52] which subsequently recommended no action.

Once again the commissioned church workers (171 in number: 146 of them women and 25 men) were denied the right to vote. After 1966 no further attempt was made on behalf of the commissioned church workers. Each year their number dwindles, and according to the 1974 report there are 134 commissioned church workers: 114 women and 20 men.[53] Their present "state of mind" about themselves and their status in the church is described in detail in the following chapter.

The Ordination of Women as Ministers

Many attempts to secure for women the privilege of ordination to the gospel ministry were made in the early decades of this century, culminating in the overtures presented to the General Assembly in 1929. At that time only the overture permitting the ordination of women as elders was approved by the presbyteries and added to the Form of Government in 1930. From that time on there was sporadic discussion of the issue, but no real movement to bring it again before the church until 1953. That year the Presbytery of Rochester overtured the General Assembly "to initiate such actions as may be necessary to permit the ordination of women to the Ministry of Jesus Christ." [54]

In its customary fashion, the General Assembly appointed a Special Committee on the Ordination of Women to study the matter. This committee, consisting of four ruling elders, two men and two women, and three clergymen, first reviewed the report of United Church Women concerning the place of women in the ministry of all denominations. Subsequently, the committee decided to institute further studies in three areas: (1) the Biblical texts dealing with the subject, (2) the Reformed faith "as a doctrinal guide to practice," and (3) "the present social and economic conditions as they affect the position of women in our society." [55]

The committee's report, as presented to the Assembly two years later in 1955, contained a lengthy series of reasons for the ordination of women, the most significant of which are probably the following:

> Whereas, in the Presbyterian form of government, ordination to the ministry is the only way for a full-time church worker to participate fully and responsibly in Presbytery and in the other courts of the Church;
>
> Whereas, the ministry of our Church is becoming more and more diversified, with increasing opportunities not only for pastors and preachers, but for teachers, missionaries, directors of religious education, chaplains, social workers, and other church vocations;
>
> Whereas, the ordination of women would enable the Church to give status to women now serving the Church and would also encourage others to undertake the work of ministry. . . .[56]

The report, approved by the Assembly, concluded with the recommendation that an overture be sent to the presbyteries proposing that the sentence "Both men and women may be called to this office" be added to the Form of Government, Chapter IV, Section 1. By the time that the next General Assembly met in 1956, the presbyteries had voted overwhelmingly in favor of it (205 affirmative; 35 negative).[57] Women had won—at long last—the right to full and equal participation in the Presbyterian Church!

Considering the patient struggle waged by women in this century for full equality in the Presbyterian Church, one might speculate as to why the ordination of women was approved in 1956 with so little evidence of controversy. Correspondence with the chairman of the Special Committee on the Ordination of Women, the Rev. C. Vin White, indicates that in his judgment special attention was given by the Committee to the following: *(a)* "European churches with long histories of ordained women clergy;" *(b)* the response of several Biblical scholars in the United States and Europe concerning the Biblical teaching about the ordination of women; and *(c)* the "hurtful limitations placed upon commissioned church workers," especially those in mission fields where they were "greatly handicapped by not having been ordained as clergy." [58] Another member of the committee, the Rev. Frank McCormick, wrote: "Our Committee assumed a broad and contemporary interpretation of Scripture and took St. Paul at his word—'There are neither male nor female in Christ' (Galatians 3:28) assuming that what he said was inspired by the Holy Spirit and not a contradiction of the Gospel of Christ; not just double talk." [59] Dr. Hermann N. Morse, then General Secretary of the Board of National Missions, believes that the ordination of women at that particular time was primarily "an idea whose time had come." [60]

Undoubtedly many factors entered into the situation, not the least of which was the attitude of Dr. Eugene Carson Blake. At that time he was Stated Clerk of the General Assembly (and customarily considered the most powerful individual in the structure of the Presbyterian Church). He also served as consultant to the Special Committee. According to Dr. Margaret Shannon, who served as an executive with the Commission on Ecumenical Mission and Relations and worked closely with Dr. Blake, he knew of a somewhat traumatic and embarrassing experience at the end of World War II in relation to ordained women clergy. The incident is described here to indicate the variety of forces that sometimes affect the course of history, including church history.

In 1946 the first civilian permitted to leave Japan and enter the United States was the Rev. Mrs. Tamaki Uemura, an ordained minister of the Church of Christ in Japan of which the Presbyterian Church was part. She came on the invitation of United Presbyterian Women and was scheduled to speak at their National Meeting in Grand Rapids, Michigan. A Communion service was to be celebrated at the meeting, and permission was requested to allow her to take part as one of the officiating clergy. If she had been a man, there would have been no problem. But permission was denied by the Stated Clerk, William B. Pugh, on the grounds that women could not be ordained in the Presbyterian Church. However, Mrs. Uemura was a day late in arriving at the meeting, and the Communion service had already taken place. It was agreed, under the circumstances, that she would not need to be embarrassed by being told of the negative decision. But an article appeared in *The Christian Century* reporting the incident. Consequently, a few weeks later, Mrs. Uemura heard of it. She is reported to have thought a moment, and then said: "Oh, I think I will go around creating more commotion. God, give me wisdom." [61]

In assessing the action of the General Assembly in 1956, one needs to keep in mind also that this was a

"MEN AND WOMEN MAY BE CALLED TO THIS OFFICE" 137

time of rising religious interest, with increasing church membership and high optimism in the church. Birthrates were skyrocketing. The "feminine mystique" of "home and family" was at its height.[62] Economic expansion was bringing affluence to millions. The "cold war" with the Soviet Union and Senator Joseph McCarthy's hunt for Communists in high places added to the excitement of the times, as well as bringing about a kind of numbing conformity. The church found itself striving to respond to the times by establishing thousands of new churches in suburbia and adding personnel to the staffs of local churches so that they could serve the influx of new families.

This was a time when the ordination of women as ministers did not pose a threat to the already established clergy, for there were hundreds of vacancies for both ordained and unordained professionals. As the committee's report indicated, there was the prospect of ever-expanding forms of ministry. With the apostle Paul's writings reinterpreted, and with churches crying for trained leadership, what valid reason did the church have for denying ordination to women? Indeed, this was "an idea whose time had come."

6

THE RISE AND FALL OF A POWER BASE

> In my own experience as a director of Christian education, I was led, after two years of trying to keep Christian education from being one compartment of church life, to seek ordination. I wanted to be a minister so that I would have the right to say that education was part of everything that happened in a Christian congregation where Christ was equipping his people for their service in the world.[1]
>
> Rev. Letty M. Russell
> in Christian Education in Mission

Shadows of orange-leaved maples flitted across the gray stones of First Presbyterian Church, Syracuse, New York. It was an October Sunday in

1956. A former medical photographer at the Mayo Clinic was being ordained a minister of the gospel. What made this ordination historic was the fact that this minister was the first woman to be ordained in the Presbyterian Church in the U.S.A. Thirty-one-year-old Margaret Towner had been graduated in 1953 from Union Seminary in New York with a Bachelor of Divinity degree, taken because she "felt that only by taking the same courses as a future pastor would I receive adequate training as a Christian educator." [2] From the write-up of this occasion in the denominational magazine, *Presbyterian Life*, it would appear that the Rev. Miss Towner was less impressed with the breakthrough that she had made than with the possibilities of serving as a kind of model for Christian educators.

No cheering here for the achievement of equal ecclesiastical rights, though equality had been gained, at least in theory. No trumpeting for equal opportunity even. Rather, here was the unconscious assumption that women were primarily educators in the church, and acceptance of that role as both desirable and significant.

While difficult to document, the attitude of Miss Towner toward herself as essentially an educator, even though ordained, was apparently characteristic of the women who were ordained in the period between 1956 and 1960. This was probably because many of them had been serving as directors of Christian education before ordination, and religious education was riding a crest of popularity in the church.

A Power Base Takes Shape

Christian Education Takes Hold

As has been noted in Chapter 5, the religious education movement in its earlier years (prior to 1950) never made a dramatic impact on the program of the Presbyterian Church. Religious education was accepted as important and tolerated as a necessary function of every congregation, but religious educators did not hold much power in the councils of the church.

But in the 1940's several developments took place which began to change this picture. In 1942 women in missionary societies and others formed the Presbyterian Women's Organization nationally, and recommended that all women's groups in local churches become "inclusive." This meant that a single Women's Association be organized superseding the former Women's Missionary Societies and Ladies' Aid Societies. These associations were asked to give support not only to the two mission boards but also to the work of the Board of Christian Education.

At about the same time, Presbyterians decided to pull out of the Christian Endeavor movement and form their own young people's organization, known as Westminster Fellowship. The Westminster Fellowship National Council was formed in 1944 at Lakeside, Ohio, made up of youth representatives from all the synods of the church.[3] Following this development, the Board of Christian Education, which was designated by the General Assembly to provide staff services and resourcing for Westminster Fellowship, undertook a series of regional institutes to train directors of Christian education and pastors in a new approach to youth work.[4]

The year 1942 was also the time when a new curriculum was conceived. At an extended conference at Wagner College on Staten Island, Christian educators from across the country met to consider a totally new approach to teaching in the church school. Here the fundamental principles for the *Christian Faith and Life* curriculum were hammered out, based on the conviction that there must be a partnership between the church and the home. It was agreed that one hour (or less) of Sunday school per week was completely inadequate for teaching the fundamentals of faith. Therefore, in the new approach to Christian education, the responsibility of parents was to be highlighted, with resource materials provided. In addition, there was to be a new emphasis on theology and church history. The curriculum was planned around a three-year cycle: one year on Jesus Christ, one on the Bible, and one on the church.[5] Dr. James D. Smart of Canada (later professor of Biblical history at Union Theological Seminary) was brought to Philadelphia to head up a completely new staff of editors. (Interestingly, all but one of the age group editors were women. The one male editor was related to junior highs.) For the next six years the Board of Christian Education poured its energies and two million dollars into the *Christian Faith and Life* curriculum, launching it in the churches in 1948.[6]

To introduce this new educational venture to local

churches, the Board of Christian Education, under whose aegis the curriculum was developed and distributed, set up an intensive program of leadership education. Training schools and workshops for pastors and directors of Christian education, for church school teachers and superintendents, for elders and members of Christian education committees in local churches were held across the country.

A significant development took place at this time in relation to women religious educators, according to the Rev. W. H. Vernon Smith, who was field director for Christian education in Pennsylvania, then the largest synod of the church. The fundamental concepts involved in the new curriculum were heavily theological (neo-orthodox). As a result, many Christian educators, whose previous training and experience had been largely "process-oriented" rather than "content-centered," found themselves in unfamiliar territory. Conversely, many ordained men, who heretofore had often relegated Christian education to women, began to be interested in this field. Dr. James Smart, first editor in chief of the *Christian Faith and Life* curriculum, wrote a book entitled *The Church Must Teach—Or Die*, which added impetus to the growing respectability of Christian education. Across the church, many local pastors began to take a fresh look at their religious education programs. As a consequence of the training institutes and the widespread publicity about the new curriculum, Christian education by 1950 became the most dynamic program area in the Presbyterian Church.[7]

The Birth of NADCE

During this period, the term "director of religious education" in local churches was almost synonymous with a woman. As has been noted above, the various schools of religious education had begun as training schools for women. Even when these same schools merged with seminaries, both students and faculty in the Christian education departments were mostly women.

As the new curriculum began to give new impetus to Christian education in the church, and as directors of Christian education began to feel more confident of their role in the church with the upgrading of the commissioned church worker status in 1948 (see Chapter 5), there grew a demand for some kind of professional fellowship. In Illinois an informal association of professional church educators, known as DOPES (Directors of Presbyterian Education), was organized.[8] In the metropolitan area of New York a similar group was formed.

During this period the International Council of Religious Education held annual meetings for the purpose of assisting Christian educators to keep abreast of new ideas and new approaches to their work. Many congregations included an item in their annual budgets to enable their director of religious education to attend these meetings. In the late 1940's the Presbyterians attending the International Council meetings began to meet informally. At one such gathering in Columbus in 1947 with the Rev. Hamlin Tobey, then field director of Christian education in

Ohio, it was decided to meet the following year a day prior to the ICRE meeting.[9] With the exception of Harry Adamson of Topeka, Kansas, Jack McCracken of Chicago, and a few male staff members of the Board of Christian Education, these meetings—which were held for the next several years—were composed almost entirely of women.[10] In 1949, the National Association of Directors of Christian Education, known as NADCE, was born. Fifty-nine women and thirteen men joined as charter members.[11] The purpose was to provide a channel for communication throughout the year.

Even though by far the majority of the members were women, interestingly and predictably, they chose a man, Harry Adamson, to be chairman and Hamlin Tobey to be staff consultant. According to Vernon Smith, this action may have been an intuitive recognition that as women they needed as their spokesmen men who had access to power.[12]

Because of the importance of Christian education in the life of the Presbyterian Church during the early 1950's, NADCE grew in numbers, and gradually became "equal to any other power base in the church at that time," in the view of Vernon Smith.[13] The only other power base of any consequence was the Presbyterian Women's Organization, which derived its "clout" from the financial support that it gave to the program of the church.[14]

With Christian education firmly established as one of the most significant areas of the church's program, increasingly a somewhat larger number of male seminary students began taking courses in this field. Jobs were plentiful, for it will be remembered that this was a time of increasing membership and enthusiastic optimism in the major denominations. Quite naturally, those who took jobs in this field following graduation joined the association for professional religious educators and began attending their meetings regularly. This development delighted many of the women in the association, who saw in this movement a validation of the importance of their own work.[15] By 1959, at the meeting of NADCE, there were 115 men and 178 women present.[16] By 1962, when the association met in St. Louis, there were more men than women in attendance.[17] From that time on, there have been more men than women on the Executive Committee, with only three women out of twelve officers elected in 1972.[18]

Christian Education in Decline

What Happened and How?

To determine exactly what happened in the professional Christian education field during the 1940's and 1950's is something like piecing together the clues of a detective story. The records that might have been used to uncover what happened in the past two decades in relation to professional Christian educators have been either lost or destroyed.[19] Therefore, a survey of 203 churches known to have traditionally employed staff persons responsible for Christian education programs was conducted by the author. From

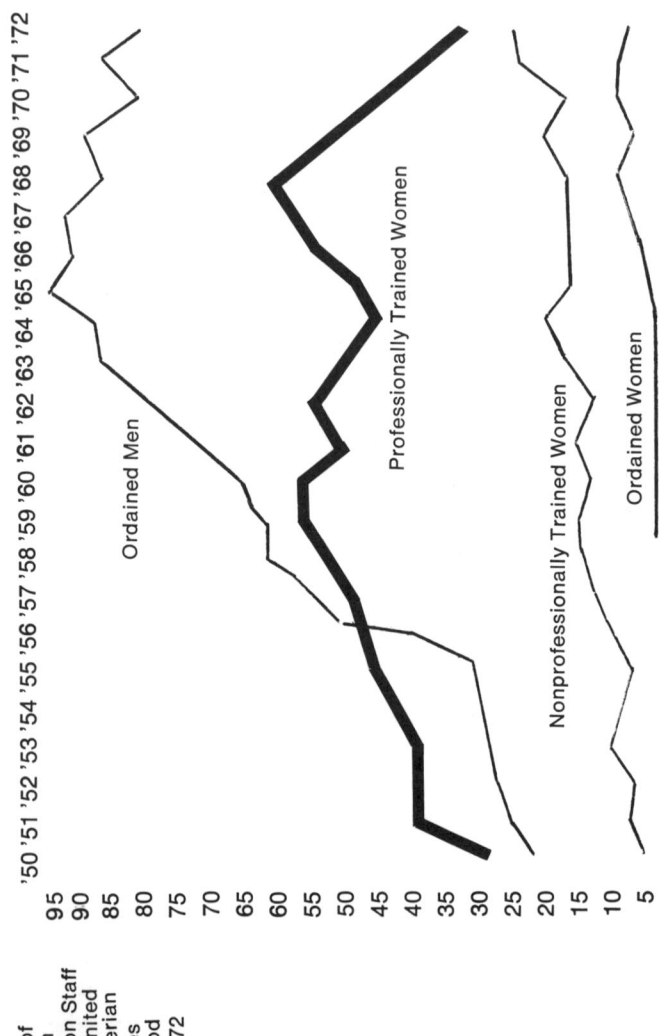

the 153 churches responding, all areas of the country were covered and the memberships of the churches ranged from 401 to 7,320.[20] When the reply from every local church responding was charted, it became evident that the number of professionally trained women in Christian education positions exceeded the number of ordained men only in the period from 1950 to 1956, with the number of men increasing rapidly and steadily from 1954 to 1965. In 1959 another significant change occurred. In the chart the *direction* of the line for ordained men is seen to continue its upward climb, while the *direction* of the line for professionally trained women begins an almost steady decline.

The chart also indicates that from 1968 on, when a general "budget squeeze" began to take effect, the number of ordained men declined somewhat, but the number of professionally trained women began to plunge. Concomitant with this is the corresponding rise in the number of nonprofessionally trained women. The line for ordained women shows a slight increase since 1965, but the number is so small as to be negligible.

Implications of the Study

Certainly it can be said that in the 153 churches responding to the survey the professionally trained woman in the '70s is caught in a "double squeeze" as far as jobs are concerned—between ordained men and nonprofessionally trained women. Because of the general decrease in membership throughout the denomination (a reported loss of 104,000 members during 1972 continues a trend first reported in 1966), a generally unsettled economic situation in the nation with correspondingly smaller church budgets reported for the most part, it could be that professionally trained women are being replaced by ordained men because of the additional functions that they perform acceptably—preaching, calling, counseling, etc. Also, it may indicate that those churches which want to have a full-time staff person responsible for Christian education cannot afford the higher salaries that professionally trained women usually command and therefore turn to an ex-public school teacher or some other laywoman in their congregations to take this position. Comments on a number of the survey questionnaires seem to bear this out. Nevertheless, a preference for a woman in the Christian education field was indicated by some.

Many subtle elements are involved. The prevailing attitude of the senior pastor (to whom the questionnaires were addressed), past experience with particular men and women, and the attitude of the responder toward education itself, make it impossible to be precise in analyzing exactly what happened in the Christian education movement in the Presbyterian Church. In order to gain insight from the commissioned church workers themselves, the author circulated a questionnaire in January 1972, to all the commissioned church workers listed in the 1971 copy of the Minutes of the General Assembly. This list was composed of 131 women and 20 men. There were 92 replies, many with comments and notations added.

The results indicate certain ambiguities. For example, 46 women feel that commissioning has helped them in their careers, while 51 women do not believe that it was essential in securing their present jobs. But the overall results do not indicate overwhelming support for or satisfaction with the status of commissioned church worker. Commissioning is considered useful by only 15 women and 7 men, with 48 women and 3 men responding in the negative.

The comments indicate that one of the major complaints is that commissioned church workers have no vote in presbytery, as the following excerpts show:[21]

> I think the inability to vote [in presbytery] rankles me most. An ordained session member can vote at presbytery with no theological training, but I am not allowed to. And they call women illogical!
>
> A CCW should have a vote in presbytery. I have a voice supposedly, but I am not going to speak, and then sit dumbly by when the vote is taken.

Another point of resentment, mentioned by 40 women respondents, is related to salary discrimination:

> Always an embarrassed laugh when salary or status (is) introduced in Sessions, but no move to face reality and tackle the problem. . . . Not only the fact of being a woman, but that of being unmarried and having no children contributed to the absolute refusal of pastors or congregations to look at poverty wages.
>
> The first church I served could not possibly find the

money to raise my salary. When I left they hired a single man at $2000 additional salary. I was supporting my mother at the time and could not live on the salary I was receiving.

Probably the most significant finding is the response to those questions relating to the shift in leadership in the Christian education field from women to men. (Interestingly enough, none of the men responded to these questions.) Of the 50 women who did, 43 indicated their belief that a shift did occur, especially in local churches. Half the respondents believe that this shift in leadership from women to men occurred in the period from 1960 to 1964, or shortly thereafter. This is the same time frame indicated in the study of 200 local congregations described above.

Within the limitations of these two studies, then, it can be stated with some certainty that in the United Presbyterian Church the Christian education movement saw a change in membership and in leadership in the early 1960's, with men continuing in the positions of power in the judicatories and boards—which they had always held—but assuming those roles in the professional organization of Christian educators, and in local churches.

Demoralization and Defense

From the responses to the questionnaires it is apparent that the commissioned church workers who responded feel a high degree of frustration and a low level of morale. Almost every one of the replies, from both men and women, somewhere reveals anxiety and disappointment. A few of the respondents wanted to make it quite clear that they also find satisfaction and fulfillment in their work, but the overall picture is certainly negative.

Another recent attempt to evaluate the status of the commissioned church worker was a study made by Miss Harriet Prichard in 1964–1965, when she was vice-president of TAUPCE (The Association of United Presbyterian Church Educators, a new name for NADCE). At that time, she wrote a paper entitled "Some Practical Reflections on 'The Nature of the Ministry' Report." [22] In this paper Miss Prichard vividly describes the problems of the Christian educator and of the commissioned church worker in particular:

> The title "Commissioned Church Worker" means a lot of things to a lot of people. To some it means professional church educator, but to others it means "church drudge," "Sunday school bracero," and many other things not worth mentioning. The title "CCW" has been given to so many different functions in the church (Director of Music, Board Staff Executive, teacher, doctor, nurse) that the idea of educator is not singular or unique at all when connected with this ecclesiastical jargon. People in the pews do not know what it is all about! The title is a title in limbo—it connotes neither "clergy" nor "laity." It does not define the job being accomplished. It is a worthless specification, and *The Report* does well to ask for its abolishment. Certainly better titles are not difficult to discover. . . .

What is the "CCW" then? He or she is a competent educator (social worker, musician, or doctor) with special training in Bible and theology. The "CCW" in education has passed the Presbytery examination which allows him or her to engage in an educational ministry (but many are engaged in this ministry who have not passed such an examination!) and he or she has been installed—but nothing more! There is no committee of Presbytery that continues to care about the CCW's work, that helps him or her to continue his or her education or that protects him or her from malpractice in the local church. Besides this, the CCW is without vote in the Presbytery, the body that each one is required to serve faithfully. The CCW cannot enjoy a degree of understanding, for of all of the tasks in the church his or hers is the most ill-defined.[23]

Miss Prichard concludes by outlining the needs of commissioned church workers "if they are to continue their work and if they are to accomplish a significant mission for the sake of Christ's Church in the future" as follows:

They need a new title, they need to be commissioned, they need a vote, they need job security, and they need continuing education.[24]

A questionnaire was sent out with the above paper to all the members of TAUPCE, numbering 1800. The church educators were requested to read the paper and the *Report of the Special Committee on the Nature of the Ministry,* printed in a church professional magazine, and then to return the questionnaire. Two hundred fifty-eight (14.3 percent) of the church educators responded. A special conference of twenty educators from all parts of the country met for a week in the summer of 1965 to study the replies and to make their own report, which was then sent to the Committee on the Nature of the Ministry. The conference, on the basis of its analysis of the replies, proposed that local churches elect a group of "teaching elders" similar to the ordering of church offices first outlined by John Calvin.[25]

The Committee on the Nature of the Ministry had been at work for seven years when this proposal came to it at its final meeting in November 1965. But according to the Minutes of that meeting, the Prichard paper and the report of the TAUPCE Conference were not considered by the whole committee, but were delegated to one of the members for later report.

It may be instructive to try to speculate about what really happened in the matter of the Prichard papers. They were obviously too late to be accorded the consideration due them. When pressed on the point as to whether or not they would have been given detailed consideration if received earlier, Dr. Fred Maier, staff consultant, replied that they would have received consideration but the proposals would not have been accepted, since the Committee felt already overburdened in trying to deal with ordination, and certainly would have been in no mood to take on a full-scale consideration of "commissioning" which many people "considered to be a mistake that the church had made." [26]

But why were the papers so late? Were the Christian educators remiss or lazy or uninterested?

What motivated them to action at the eleventh hour? Discussion with many Christian educators of that period leads to the speculation that they suddenly saw their hard-won status evaporating in the mists of the ministry issue, and so they took action to save their office.

It is also possible that there was another, more subtle, dimension involved in this action. There may have been a kind of unarticulated resentment that they, as professional church workers, had not been included as participants in the Nature of the Ministry seminars, which were organized in 1962 across the country to consider the meaning of ordination. While not a conscious exclusion, exclusion it was! As professional Christian educators they did not qualify either as pastors or as lay persons. They felt that therefore their voice had not been heard by the Nature of the Ministry Committee as indeed it had not.

At this point in time it is impossible to ascertain whether or not the fact that most of the Christian educators were women had anything at all to do with the way the Prichard paper and the report were dealt with. These were the years of the civil rights struggle in America, and the church was absorbed in it. Betty Friedan's milestone book *The Feminine Mystique* did not hit the bookstands until 1964, and the question about women's role in the church was not yet a conscious issue.

This unconsciousness about women is reflected over and over in the Minutes of the Committee on the Nature of the Ministry. It should be recalled that the

Presbyterian Church had voted to ordain women to the ministry in 1956. But the language of the Minutes, with one or two exceptions, is completely male-oriented. Whether there was actually a lack of consciousness on the part of Committee members concerning women in the ministry, or whether these members were using masculine language "generically" is a debatable question.

In any event, the Christian educators, mostly women, were left out of the Nature of the Ministry seminars, and then when they found that their ecclesiastical status was in jeopardy, they rallied to action. But the action was too little and too late, and the proposals were probably too lacking in realism.

In 1966 the Report of the Nature of the Ministry Committee was accepted by the General Assembly, and the committee dismissed. Since that time, various groups within the Christian education professional organization (TAUPCE and now APCE—Association of Presbyterian Christian Educators) have been working on proposals to upgrade the status of both commissioned church workers and church educators.[27] Some changes are in the offing.

The Decline

This chapter has described the rise of Christian education as a powerful force in the Presbyterian Church in the 1940's and 1950's. With it came the formation of a power base in the National Association of Directors of Christian Education, the majority of whom were women. In addition, it has shown that this center of power was never developed as a power base *for women,* even though potentially it might have been.

A number of factors presumably entered into the failure of the women to capitalize on the potential that NADCE held for them. First, it should be remembered that this was the era of the "feminine mystique."[28] Reared in the tradition that identity and fulfillment are derived from relationship to men, most career women had no such primary relationship. The majority of career women were unmarried, and may have turned to male colleagues to fill this gap.

Another factor may have been, as already mentioned, that women Christian educators realized that power in the church was wielded primarily by men. Therefore, to gain power themselves they were content to use the channels of power already established.

A third element probably had its origin in the fact that directors of Christian education tended to believe that religious education was a "stepchild" of the church, and that the teaching ministry was somehow inferior to the preaching ministry. When men began to show up at their meetings and take part as equals, the women courted their participation by assigning them leadership roles. By this means, the women not only validated their own work in Christian education as significant, but also assured a continuing partnership.

For these reasons, and perhaps for others that are not so evident, the women Christian educators chose not to develop the power that they had. Co-opting men into their movement, the women failed to maintain the necessary balance of power that successful co-optation requires. Instead they lost their power to the group that they had co-opted. As Selznick points out in his descriptions of co-optation, this is always one of the risks that is involved in any co-optation.[29]

This loss of power by the women educators, coupled with other forces in the 1960's, signaled the beginning of the decline of Christian education in the Presbyterian Church. The spotlight that had focused so brightly yet so briefly on Christian education moved to the social activists. Education was no longer viewed as the most promising path to success, peace, or enlightenment.

In the Presbyterian Church, many of the younger men who previously had elected to train for Christian education work became deeply involved in community organization and social action projects. Women, on the whole, tended to feel uncomfortable in such a revolutionary milieu. As a consequence, they were left to mind the school.

This division of Christian educators into two relatively unhostile camps, i.e., the social activist men and the education-oriented women, fragmented the Christian education movement within the church. As a result, when the more conservative branch of the church began to assert itself in the late '60s, with its call for a more evangelistic emphasis, there was not sufficient unity and power among religious educators to meet the challenge. This brought about a reduction of budgets, both locally and nationally. Directors of

Christian education were the first professional staff persons to be eliminated by congregations, as has been demonstrated above in the survey of churches.

The Aftermath

With the decline of Christian education in the Presbyterian Church came then a decrease in the number of professional women employed in the field. Since there are fewer Christian education positions open, it has become increasingly difficult for a woman trained in Christian education to find a job. The few jobs open are most often filled by ordained men who can function, as noted above, in a variety of roles. The day of the specialist in Christian education appears to have passed, or is at least in eclipse.

Another dimension in the picture has been noted by nearly every person interviewed by the author.[30] It is a dimension that is impossible to document other than through observation and experience. It is the dimension of *quality*. In the heyday of Christian education the women who were involved in leadership roles as editors and program secretaries in the Board of Christian Education, as well as many of the local church directors of Christian education and women serving on university campuses, were women of outstanding ability and acumen. Several interviewees have asked the question: Where today are the Margaret Hummels, the Dorothy Fritzes, the Julia Tottens, and others like Jean MacDougal, Miriam Jones, Myrl Jean Hughes, Jean Stewart, and Neva Palmeter? Is the dearth of their kind due to the fact that women of their quality have, since 1956, chosen ordination only to find the road to responsibility blocked? Or is it perhaps because the decline of Christian education has created a situation in which women of ability simply do not find this field attractive and significant? Whatever the reason, the fact remains.

7

"IN CHRIST THERE IS NEITHER MALE NOR FEMALE" ... BUT IN THE PRESBYTERIAN CHURCH?

> The Task Force calls women to take on the responsibilities of freedom, to give strength and courage to each other, and to trust the movement and power of God's spirit in the world. The Task Force calls men to think on these things and to seek their own liberation from the idols of our time.
>
> *Report of the Standing Committee on Women to the 183d General Assembly, May 1971*

This has been a story of patience, tact, resilience, and perseverance. Shifting its focus from time to time, the story has moved from women with a desire for recognition to women who demanded equality and got it. Discovering that equality does not guarantee power, Presbyterian women, after struggling for decades, are now engaged in a new search for understanding of both equality and power.

A Retrospective View

Presbyterian women came together early in the nineteenth century to put their concern for the poor and the pagan into concrete form. They sent Bibles and tracts to missionaries on the field. They sewed garments for needy ministerial students. They collected money for "missions." Eventually, they established schools and hospitals where there were none. The ministry and witness of these women expanded with the needs of a building nation.

By 1873 the potential power of these Presbyterian women was recognized by the pioneer home missionary, Sheldon Jackson. As a result, he solicited their assistance and a firm alliance was formed, aided by certain other men such as Dr. Henry Kendall, head of the Board of Home Missions. This alliance brought a measure of recognition and respect to the women, who subsequently organized themselves into the Woman's Board of Home Missions.

Incorporated in 1915, the Woman's Board was granted the status of an "Assembly Board," reporting directly to the General Assembly. With a budget of $1,068,091,[1] with 451 missionaries working in 78 stations,[2] with 24 boarding schools and 8 hospitals,[3] the program of the Woman's Board of Home Missions in the last year of its existence (1923) constituted one of the most widespread, most dramatic, and most carefully administered aspects of home missions work in the Presbyterian Church at that time.[4] Over the years the Board of Home Missions had turned to the Woman's Board on more than one occasion for financial assistance during lean years. Frequently the General Assembly had commended the women for their responsible stewardship. Commitment, diligent administration, and genuine, concerned generosity on the part of the women had won them not only the recognition that they desired but a true power base in the church as well.

But with restlessness and change infecting the whole of society during the 1920's, the church was not immune. Change was the order of the day, so that the women's exercise of power was destined to be short-lived. By 1922 the General Assembly, after deliberating for several years, determined that all the former thirteen boards and agencies were to be consolidated into four Boards, with the Woman's Board of Home Missions merged into the Board of National Missions as a special department of educational and medical work. The women concurred with this action reluctantly.

There is no evidence to suggest that the officers and staff of the Woman's Board of Home Missions resisted consolidation on the grounds that they would lose their power center. In fact, there is little to suggest that they were even aware that they had a power base. Rather, they resisted the change because they feared that without the continuing, personalized nurture of their educational and medical ventures on the mission field and without the constant promotion of the extra "second-mile" giving from women's groups, those missionary organizations would die. If that happened. the mission program that they had so zealously built up over the years would cease to exist. At the outset, the women leaders did not see consolidation in terms of a loss of power for themselves as women. Rather, they saw it as a loss of control over a particular kind of missionary program to which they were committed.

Within a few short years, however, the women became more conscious of what had really happened in the reorganization process. Their original fears had not been realized. Their schools and hospitals were still operating. Their missionary groups were still flourishing across the church. On that score there was no complaint. What nettled women leaders such as Mrs. Katharine Bennett, former president of the Woman's Board of Home Missions, and Miss Margaret Hodge, former president of the Woman's Board of Foreign Missions, was the injustice of the General Assembly action forcing them to give up control of their mission program. Since no women were permitted to participate as voting members of General Assembly at that time, no woman had taken part in this decision. Too late, these women leaders had recognized that they had had a real power base *as women.* Too late they recognized that, with no woman eligible to vote in any part of the denominational structure beyond the local congregation, there was not much that they could have done about the consolidation. Their power structure, built up over the years with the assistance of a number of influential men, had been co-opted. Viewed in the light of Selznick's definition of co-optation, the Board of National Missions had absorbed several "new elements into its leadership" [5] and policy-making, among them the Woman's Boards. This was done perhaps as a means "of establishing the legitimacy of the authority" [6] of the General Assembly's program of home missions, and as a way of "signifying participation in the process of decision and administration." [7] According to the definition described in Chapter 1, one could say that formal co-optation had taken place.

Smarting from what had happened, some of the women leaders sought redress by working for the right to vote in Presbyterian decision-making bodies like the General Assembly. But since only the ordained could vote in the judicatories of the church, the women had first to win the right to ordination. That struggle continued for over thirty years, with ordination for women elders being approved in 1930, and for ordination to the ministry in 1956.

In this first instance of co-optation, then, women's taking responsibility for mission work led to recognition and respect by the church. By building up this work, the women gained an institutional foothold, which was in turn co-opted by the church structures in the consolidation of the boards in 1923. The women's response to co-optation gave birth to a demand for equality, which was ultimately granted. But, as has been shown, the gaining of equality by women did not restore them to power.

The second example of co-optation, related to the religious education movement in the Presbyterian Church, is more complex. The power center established by Christian educators in the 1940's included both men and women, though women were definitely in the majority. Also, as a power base, while solid and real, it was never openly acknowledged as such by the church. In this instance, it was the women themselves who initiated the co-opting process, for the women religious educators not only welcomed men into leadership positions but sought them out. As a consequence, the women religious educators permitted the co-opted element, i.e., the men, to take over, to "take advantage of their position and encroach on actual areas of decision." [8] According to Selznick's description of co-optation, the women in this case did not exercise the "informal control over the coopted elements" [9] that would have preserved their power.

If this analysis is correct, then one of the major reasons for the women's failure to control their power may have been due to a lack of understanding that they did indeed *have* a power center. Or, it may have been because they failed to think of themselves first as women, and second as religious educators. For the most part, evidence suggests that they were more concerned about the place and power of religious education in the life of the church than they were in gaining recognition of themselves as women. Regardless of the cause, the fact remains that the women did lose control of the Christian education movement in the Presbyterian Church by the late 1950's.

In summary, then, this study has documented the thesis stated in Chapter 1. In the two instances in the twentieth century when women established a power base in the Presbyterian Church, the reality and effectiveness of that power structure was lost through the process of co-optation. In the first instance the power base of the women, the Woman's Board of Home Missions, was co-opted by the structure of the church, that is, the General Assembly. In the second example, the women were the co-opters. But they allowed the process to go too far, thus losing their control.

In the description of how this co-optive process developed, it has been demonstrated that professionally trained women have not been able to achieve full equality in the church. Defining a "professionally trained woman" as one whose certification and credentials are established by the General Assembly or other judicatory beyond the local church, this study has shown that the first co-optation rallied women leaders in 1927–1929 to seek ordination to the ministry, which had been repeatedly denied them. Not until 1938 was there a "professionally trained" status open to women, i.e., that of commissioned church worker. Since 1956, when ordination to the ministry was finally approved, women have found it difficult to find pastorates, a situation persisting to the present.

"IN CHRIST THERE IS NEITHER MALE NOR FEMALE"

*Who, What, Where, When,
and How—and Now the WHY?*

Sorting out the strands of a historic struggle, discovering the main actors and, in this case, actresses, and reconstructing the major events in such a struggle have proved both fruitful and fascinating. Such an account, it is hoped, has validity in and of itself without further elaboration.

But in the deeper recesses of the mind there always lurks the question Why? *Why* did Presbyterian women understand so early the legitimacy of educational and medical work as an extension of evangelism? *Why* was Sheldon Jackson the only man to work so diligently to help the women organize nationally? Was it not possible that his own ends could have been served as well by some other means? *Why* did the women leaders of the Woman's Board of Home Missions capitulate so readily in the merger of the boards in 1922?

In the instance of the religious education movement, *why* were the women involved in that movement so reticent to assume leadership themselves, and at the same time, so ready to co-opt men into leadership roles? When the only professional status open to women Christian educators, i.e., that of commissioned church worker, was so unsatisfactory, *why* did they resist so ineffectually? *Why* did they fail to consolidate their power base, and, instead, permit male Christian educators to take control? *Why* did TAUPCE wait to understand the implications of the

Nature of the Ministry study in 1958–1965 until it was too late to affect the outcome?

In the writing of this book, all these questions have been raised and dealt with to some extent. But speculative answers to these specific questions provoke the mind to deeper questioning of a more generalized Why?

Why, for example, did Presbyterian men, particularly the clergy, resist for so long the claim to equality on the part of women of the church—a claim that was recognized by society in the granting of suffrage and in other professional fields long before? Why, even now that ecclesiastical equality has been approved, do women ministers find it so difficult to secure and maintain pastoral positions commensurate with their training and abilities? Is there validity in the observation that frequently it is laywomen themselves who seem most prejudiced against calling an ordained woman as pastor of their church? If so, why is this the case—especially in view of the fact that women constitute well over half the membership of most major denominations, including the Presbyterian? And, finally, why have Presbyterian women used the power that they already had so ineffectively? Is there something perhaps in the nature of women themselves that is a deterrent to wielding power well?

Obviously, questions like these do not yield to exact answers. With the evidence presently available, they are speculative questions and as such engender only further speculation. They involve affective factors rooted in history, in culture, and in psychology, all of which are intermingled in a complex network. Therefore, the best that can be done is to examine these forces briefly in the hope that they may spark further inquiry.

Historical and Cultural Forces

Given the history of Western civilization with its patriarchal system and the history of the Christian church with its male-dominated hierarchy, it is no wonder that women found little equality or power until the last hundred years. Higher education was available only for males until the middle of the nineteenth century. Exploration of vast new territories presented rigors for which women were not prepared. Business and industry demanded abilities and skills that women had not developed (except the ability to work long hours in the sweatshops of England and the American Northeast). Rather, women's role in society was proscribed, precise, and accepted. They were childbearers, nurturers of the family, and helpmeets for their husbands. Any deviation from this norm was unacceptable to both men and women.

Both culturally and historically (for the two can hardly be separated), these prescribed roles have given rise to certain observable characteristics, sometimes labeled "feminine" and "masculine." Generally speaking, men are expected to be adventurous, aggressive, virile, physically strong, and competitive. Women, on the other hand, are to be protective, passive, compliant, and concerned for others.

These characteristics, then, were expressive of the

roles for men and women demanded in society. And at the same time, the roles were reinforced by society's expectations of these characteristics in male and female.

With the advent of equality on many fronts—education, suffrage, business, and the professions—the neat distinctions between male and female roles began to crumble. Spurred on by changes in society brought on by World War II, by changes in family life occasioned by the flight to the suburbs and laborsaving devices, the actual roles of men and women in American society have changed also. In the decade of the 1950's, the "feminine mystique" tried to reverse the trend, but the decade of the 1960's and the beginning years of the 1970's have demonstrated that this trend, for the time being at least, is alive and well.

Many women today are clamoring for equality in every sphere—in family life, in the area of sex, in sports, as well as in business, the professions, and the church. They are demanding the right to be adventurous, aggressive, strong, and competitive, if they so desire. Without a countermove on the part of men to be allowed to be protective, passive, compliant, and concerned for others if *they* so desire, the question arises—Who will become the carriers of these "feminine" qualities? Who will be concerned about the poor, the oppressed, the disadvantaged? Who will be the nurturers of humaneness, of unselfishness, of concern for others? Who in the church will take seriously the call to mission—as women have done in the past?

Perhaps this is why some commentators on the contemporary scene are calling for the liberation of both men and women from stereotyped roles so that *both* may become whatever they *are*—with no limitations on the characteristics they are expected to possess. Perhaps also this two-way liberation might free both men and women to use their natural talents to tackle the monumental problems of war, of technology, of the environment, that loom on the horizon.

As far as the history of the Christian church is concerned, personal relationships—within the family and between men and women—usually have followed the patterns of the culture in which the church is set. One possible exception has been the attempt by the church to stamp out polygamy in places like Africa and Utah, but these attempts have met with limited success.

At the same time, it must be remembered that the Christian church has its roots firmly in Hebrew culture, which is patriarchal in structure. Even Hebrew culture, however, is not "pure" but has, over the centuries, been influenced by the cultures around it. Consequently, it is not surprising to discover that many Eastern religions include stories about the creation, about a great flood, about the origin of evil, and about a virgin birth, that are not unlike those in the Old and New Testaments.

In most of these religions there is a similar thread relating to women; namely, that there somehow is a connection between women and evil. The story of Eve makes this point clearly. There is also a link between women and magic that has taken a variety of forms. Before the time of modern medicine there were in each community certain women, particularly in Europe, who had knowledge of herbs and the healing arts. Sometimes because of their special skills these women were considered by the illiterate masses to have magical powers. From that point to considering women as "witches" was a small step. Certainly the history of witchcraft in the New World bears out this relationship.

Possibly this idea stems from the "uncleanness" associated with childbirth and the menstrual cycle of women. Purification rites for women after childbirth were a definite part of Hebrew tradition. It may be that women were not allowed in the central section of the temple because they might be menstruating and would therefore defile it.

Still another dimension of the historical attitude of the church toward women may have some relationship to the religious practices of some of the early pagan traditions, which were probably sexual in nature. Some of these practices likely spilled over into ancient Judaism, as is attested by the railing of the prophet Amos, "Father and son resort to the same girl, to the profanation of my holy name" (Amos 2:7). If ancient pagan practices assigned women only a sexual role in their temples, is it not possible that part of the "collective unconscious" [10] that Jung talks about may make it difficult for male leaders to conceive of women as equal partners in the role of priest or minister?

Another aspect of this possibly unconscious attitude

may be related to the conception of God as a masculine personage. In the role of priest, a minister functions as a kind of liaison between God and the people. Is there perhaps, then, some resistance to the idea that a woman—who has generally been thought of as a sex object—can make this liaison between God, who is male, and the people?

It is interesting to note that the liturgically focused churches, such as the Roman Catholic and the Episcopal, have so far refused to allow women to become priests. Historically, in America, it has been the "free" churches such as the Congregational and the Church of Christ (Disciples) which early ordained women to the ministry. The churches of the Presbyterian and Reformed traditions, which stand liturgically somewhere between the Roman and Episcopal and the free churches, have ordained women only recently.[11]

Psychological Forces

Since the development of modern psychology, many leaders in this field have attempted to fathom the relationship between men and women and to understand the "battle of the sexes." While the scope of this study does not permit a careful examination of these various points of view, a brief look at some of them may be worthwhile as background for the questions to be raised.

In working with women patients, Freud discovered a complexity in the feminine that led him to say: "The great question . . . which I have not been able to answer despite my thirty years of research into the feminine soul, is 'What does a woman want?' " [12] His major conclusion, based on the conviction that anatomy is destiny, was that all women have one traumatic experience in common that leads to "penis-envy." [13] One of his associates, Karen Horney, emphasized the correlative to Freud's theory which is denial of the vagina. Basing her conclusion on the anxiety of the little girl over her Oedipal fantasies, Horney deduced that women coped with this anxiety by denying the existence of the vagina.[14]

A more recent psychologist, Erik Erikson, on the basis of certain experiments with boys and girls, has postulated that girls have a unique sense of "inner space" within themselves that is foreign to boys. According to him,

> the existence of a productive inner-bodily space safely set in the center of the female form and carriage has a reality superior to that of a missing organ.[15]

Otto Rank in his book, *Beyond Psychology*, sees fear as a basic component of the feminine. For him, fear in the woman is fear of man—since he has it within his power to withhold love and force separation. Man, on the other hand, does not fear woman but fears sex, because of its "irrationality" which he conceives as chaos, destruction, and death. Sex for him is brief, temporary, and emptying, whereas for the woman it can be sustained, creative, and fulfilling.[16] According to him, women find their immortality in the procreative process. Men, because their biological function in this process is "incidental and temporal," [17] seek their immortality in the environment. For this reason, historically, men have been "the doers, the creators and inventors, the architects and engineers."[18] Their creative power is turned outward to control and change nature and thus to gain immortality.

For Carl Jung, the presence of the feminine "anima" and the masculine "animus" in both men and women was the key to understanding the sexes. His observations led him to the conclusion that if the anima of the man and the animus of the woman went unrecognized, these forces could dominate the personality in destructive and demonic ways.[19]

The variety of these theories concerning masculinity and femininity serves only to demonstrate that there is no consensus among psychologists. It is therefore untenable to try to explain the Why? of individual or institutional behavior within the Presbyterian Church on the basis of these theories. But they do provide some background for the raising of certain questions.

First, is it possible that the long struggle for equality and power on the part of Presbyterian women is related to the failure or unwillingness of church leaders to recognize the sexual dimensions involved in church life? Is there, for example, a difference in the way a male clergyman relates to female and male parishioners?

Related to that is the question of whether or not there is any connection between the fact that in the Presbyterian Church most ministers are male and the majority of active members of any congregation are female. Do women find in the men who enter the ministry certain characteristics of compassion, concern, and protectiveness that are not so apparent in their husbands or fathers or brothers, and to which they respond? And, conversely, do male ministers find the ego-fulfillment in women's response more satisfying than would be the response of men? [20]

If there is any validity in the assumption that there are sexual dimensions involved in all levels of church life, and if these dimensions remain unrecognized and unconscious, then it may be fair to speculate that these factors are of significance in understanding the struggle that this study has documented.

A second question has to do with women's understanding of the nature of power and their attitude toward it. Do women perhaps shun the use of power—which is the capacity to alter consequences and to participate directly in the decision-making process—because they do not want to risk having to be responsible for those consequences? Are women, in general, more content to sit on the sidelines and observe—taking potshots at those who are making the decisions?

Frequently women, particularly churchwomen, protest that they are "not interested in power." Somehow the word seems to conjure up images of smoke-filled rooms, dirty politics, bribery, coercion, and the like. More feminine forms of power such as "clinging vine" and "femme fatale" are not so readily remembered. Women will quote such clichés as "Never underestimate the power of a woman" or "The hand that rocks the cradle rules the world" without recognizing the significant distinction between power and influence. In her book, *The Service and Status of Women in Churches*, Kathleen Bliss highlights this point:

> It is nonsense to say that women have never had any power in the Churches: they have immense power, but power in the form of influence, which is irresponsible power. . . . Women have wielded influence with very great skill over the centuries and many still prefer it to any form of responsibility which brings them out in the open.[21]

A third question has to do with how women use power when they have it. Is it possible that women really do not know how to use power effectively? If so, is it because they have had little practice in its use and consequently their strategies are ineffectual? Or, is there some basic quality in women that renders them incapable of its use?

In his history of American feminist movements, *Everyone Was Brave*, William L. O'Neil draws several conclusions that may be informative on this question:

> The striking thing about organized women was the degree to which they upheld the traditional womanly concern for altruism and benevolence, to the point where almost everything they did was justified in these terms. Men easily came together in labor unions, trade and professional associations, and political groups which frankly appealed to the members' desire for power, profit, or protection, and no one thought the less of them for it. . . .
>
> Masculine activities were self-justifying while women

had always to identify themselves with the highest moral and social good to excuse even relatively modest enterprises.[22]

In his view, radical feminism, which "was ruthlessly self-centered and potentially capable of grappling with the essential sources of women's disadvantaged state," [23] gave way in the twentieth century to social feminism with its emphasis on the good that women would do if granted equality. Thus the demand for equal rights became conditional, and when the feminists could not deliver the product, their power evaporated. The feminist leaders failed to see that what was needed was "a fundamental re-evaluation of women's role in American life," [24] rather than promises of a more just and humane society.

From O'Neil's study, the inference can be drawn that the very qualities associated with the feminine—compassion, concern for others, unselfishness—became, in the long run, the stumbling block to women's drive for equality and power.

If these comments are set alongside the story told here, it is pertinent to note that the first loss of a power base, with the subsequent move toward full participation in the church, took place in the 1920's. This was the same period that O'Neil noted as the end of an era—with social feminism having replaced the more radical feminism. Is there perhaps a kind of parallel here? During the latter years of the nineteenth century, when the more radical forces in the feminist movement were strong, Presbyterian women developed their power structure. Between 1916 and 1920, the drive for women's suffrage reached its peak. These four years were also the apex of Presbyterian women's power. It was in 1915 that the Woman's Board of Home Missions was incorporated as an autonomous board under the General Assembly, and in 1920 plans were initiated for the consolidation of the boards. Once the right to vote was won in the political sphere, feminist leaders no longer had a focus around which to rally their forces. Consequently, the movement socialized its demands, became fragmented, and lost its effectiveness. Is it not understandable, then, that in such a milieu, with a measure of independence and power already won by Presbyterian women, their leaders might have failed to be alert to the threat that the reorganization plan posed?

Another question comes out of the observation and experience of the author. To what extent is there a pattern in the ebb and flow of power, both in individual relationships and in institutional behavior? While certainly oversimplified, the rhythm seems to move as shown in the diagram on page 180.

The rhythm between those in power and the powerless seems to operate in the same pattern, whether the tensions are between blacks and whites, the rich and the poor, or men and women. For the purpose of this study, the pattern can perhaps be applied to Presbyterian women and the male-dominated church structure.

From this perspective, it would seem that Presbyterian women tried to break the power cycle in the 1920's. As an independent corporation, with their own

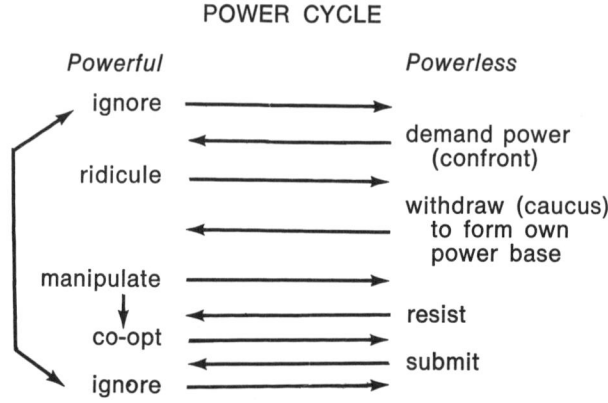

sources of income and budget, with their own property and missionaries, they negotiated from their point of power to win certain guarantees: (1) one third of the membership of the Board of National Missions; (2) administrative control over their mission program; and (3) continuation of separate women's giving. Because General Assembly recognized the women's power, these demands were granted. Having used their power successfully, the leaders of the Woman's Board of Home Missions, eager to be cooperative, fair, and unselfish, were satisfied. Concerned about the unity of the church, these women, like the social feminists of their day, were perhaps not radical enough to realize what they might have won.

Viewed in relation to the religious education movement, the power cycle was broken when the women

"IN CHRIST THERE IS NEITHER MALE NOR FEMALE" 181

religious educators misused the co-opting process. By trying to manipulate the male Christian educators into positions of leadership, the women in the movement quickly lost their control, and became, in turn, nearly powerless. Because of the "mixed" nature of the religious education movement, with both men and women involved in varying degrees, the operation of the power cycle is much less clear since neither group had total power or was powerless.

The intriguing hypothesis concerning the operation of the power cycle described above has grown out of the research for this book. It is presented here in the hope that it will engender further study and experimentation. If the hypothesis proves to be valid, it may be instructive for groups seeking power to analyze where they are in such a cycle before planning strategy.[25] At the least, this hypothesis highlights the point that the analysis of past experience stimulates the ability to generate fresh inquiry.

And the Way Ahead?

Seventy-five years have brought remarkable changes in the role of women in the Presbyterian Church:

> Women are equal ecclesiastically.
> Professionally trained women are recognized.
> Laywomen and professionally trained women are being given significant responsibilities.

But the issue of power still remains.

In the years ahead, can Presbyterian women transcend their fear of power and learn new ways of relating to church structure? Will Presbyterian clergy and laymen examine the sexual dimensions of relationship to women in the church and accept women as equal partners in practice as well as in theory? Can lay women and men cast aside old prejudices and be open to the contributions of professionally trained women? Is the current consciousness concerning women in the church merely a passing phase, or will it lead to a deeper understanding of the Christian faith in which "there is neither male nor female"? Can *both* men and women in the Presbyterian Church learn to be open to each other and thus free to serve their Lord as *persons?*

Only God knows. Only time will tell.

Appendix

Note on Women's Power in the Church

In doing the research for the above section on the treatment of the Prichard papers by the Committee on the Nature of the Ministry, the author was intrigued that no woman served at any time on that committee of General Assembly. This raised the question about the role for women on General Assembly committees generally, which prompted further study.

After the 1930 breakthrough of ordination to eldership, women were eligible, at least in theory, to serve on any of the various boards, agencies, and committees of any judicatory of the church. As has been noted above, the women membership on the Boards was spelled out in detail at the time of the 1923 consolidation. By virtue of being members of the Boards, three women became members of the General Council in 1932, and this representation has continued to the present. After the beginning of World War II a woman was appointed to membership on the Wartime Service Commission bringing to four the number of women serving on General Assembly committees.

Perhaps it is even more significant that so many of the committees of General Assembly have *never* had a woman member. These include the Permanent Judicial Commission and the Department of Ministerial Relations, both of which are prestigious and powerful groups. Other, more temporary, committees that have included no women are the Special Committee on National Purpose (1960–1961), the Special Committee on Church and State (1960–1961), the Special Committee on the Nature of the Ministry (1958–1965), the Special Committee on the Use of Drugs (1966–1970), the Special Committee on Unilateral Intervention (1966–1971), the Special Committee on the Revision of the Book of Discipline (1966–1971).

Until 1956 when ordination to the ministry was opened to women, only women who were elders were eligible to serve on General Assembly committees (unless they were elected to represent one of the Boards). It would therefore be logical to assume that after 1956 the number of women appointed to committees might be proportionately increased. Interestingly enough, however, no ordained woman minister was named to membership of any committee of General Assembly until 1967 when the Rev. Priscilla

Chaplin (who worked in the Office of General Assembly) was appointed as Alternate for Mrs. E. Harris Harbison on the Special Committee of Nine (to develop the plan for regional synods) *and* as chairman of the Special Committee on Women in Society and the Church. In fact, only *four* ordained women have served on these committees (two of them on more than one committee) and only *one* commissioned church worker (though one of the ordained women was a commissioned church worker when she served).

During the decade of the 1960's, when General Assembly was being bombarded annually with controversial issues such as civil rights, the Vietnam war, recognition of China, it is generally conceded that General Assembly and its committees wielded a good deal of power in relation to the rest of the church, i.e., determination of policy, budget, stance. Certainly it was the men of the church who made those crucial decisions, for the women on the General Assembly committees were there in token numbers only, even though women have constituted over half the membership of the denomination for years.

A study of the composition of the General Assembly committees during that decade shows that from 1961 to 1970 out of a total of 6,180 members, only 440 committee seats were held by women, or 7 percent.

Even more significant, however, was to discover that the 440 committee seats held by women during the decade studied involved *only 120* individual women. Twenty-two of the women held positions on more than one committee, and many of them were elected for three years or six years. It has been estimated that about 57 percent of the members of the United Presbyterian Church are women—or roughly speaking, over one and a half million.

Notes

Chapter 1
Encounter in the Seventies

1. This session of the General Assembly meeting was attended by the author.

2. Mary Anne Pikrone, "Her Trying Hour Before Assembly," *The Times-Union*, Rochester, N.Y., May 25, 1971, p. 19A.

3. Interview with Mrs. Lois Stair, in St. Peter, Minn., July 26, 1972.

4. Interviews with leaders of the Women's Caucus at the General Assembly meeting, May 25–26, 1971.

5. Informal meeting of leaders of the Professional Women's Caucus and others with a member of the Permanent Judicial Commission of the General Assembly, attended by the author on May 25, 1971.

6. *Ibid.*

7. *Webster's Seventh New Collegiate Dictionary* (G. & C. Merriam Company, 1963), p. 666.

8. *The Random House College Dictionary* (Random House, Inc., 1968), pp. 111–112.

9. *The Random House Dictionary of the English Language, Unabridged* (Random House, Inc., 1966), p. 1127.

10. Philip Selznick, *TVA and the Grass Roots* (University of California Press, 1949), University of California Publications in Culture and Society, Vol. III, p. 13.

11. *Ibid.*, p. 14.

12. *Ibid.*

13. *Ibid.*, p. 15.

14. *The Presbyterian Constitution and Digest*, Vol. I, "The Form of Government (Digest of the Acts, Decisions, and Deliverances of the General Assembly)" (published for the Office of the General Assembly of the Board of Christian Education, 1956), Ch. XIV, Sec. 1, p. 847.

15. Kenneth G. McCollough, "Observations from Employment Records of Ordained United Presbyterian Women," paper for Task Force on Women in the Church (1969), p. 1.

16. *Ibid.*, p. 2.

17. Letter from Covenant Presbyterian Church, Columbus, Ohio, to Miss Winsome Munro, now pastor of the United Methodist Church, Bridgeton, N.J. Letter dated May 10, 1971.

18. *Minutes of the General Assembly of The United Presbyterian Church in the United States of America*, Part III, Statistics, 1960, 1964, 1969 (Office of the General Assembly).

19. William H. Henderson, "The Professional Ministry of the United Presbyterian Church" (Board of Christian Education of The United Presbyterian Church U.S.A.), September 1971, p. 1.

20. *Ibid.*

21. *Ibid.*
22. *Ibid.,* p. 3.
23. *Ibid.*
24. *Ibid.*

25. It is difficult to compare these statistics with any degree of accuracy, since the records available on these various categories have been meager. They are presented here to indicate trends rather than absolute figures.

26. These statistics are further corroborated by a survey made in connection with this study and reported in Chapter 6.

27. Betty M. Rice, "Report of Meeting on 'Women and Church,'" *Christianity and Crisis,* Vol. XI, No. 14 (Aug. 6, 1951), p. 110.

28. Peggy Way, "Women in the Church," *Renewal,* Vol. IV, No. 7 (October 1964), p. 5.

29. *Ibid.,* p. 8.

30. Doris Cole, "Women—Church Members Second Class," *Vanguard,* Vol. IV, No. 3 (May 1967), p. 9.

Chapter 2
Benevolence Dressed in Female Form

1. *Extract from Minutes of General Assembly,* 1803–1811, p. 310.

2. Clifford M. Drury, *Presbyterian Panorama* (The Westminster Press, 1952), p. 198.

3. Margaret Gibson Hummel and Mildred Roe, *The Amazing Heritage* (The Geneva Press, 1970), p. 11.

4. Florence Hayes, *Daughters of Dorcas* (Board of National Missions, Presbyterian Church in the U.S.A., 1952), p. 141.

5. *Ibid.,* p. 142.

6. *Ibid.*, pp. 142–156.

7. *Ibid.*

8. *Ibid.*

9. *Dictionary of American Biography* (Charles Scribner's Sons, 1935), Vol. XVII, p. 521.

10. Hayes, *op. cit.*, p. 42.

11. *Dictionary of American Biography*, Vol. VII, p. 87.

12. *Ibid.*

13. *Ibid.*

14. Matilda Joslyn Gage, *Woman, Church and State* (C. H. Kerr and Co., 1893), p. 479.

15. *Ibid.*

16. Rev. George P. Hays, *May Women Speak?* (Women's Temperance Publication Association, 1889), p. 47.

17. *Ibid.*, p. 77.

18. *Ibid.*, p. 79.

19. Robert Hastings Nichols, *Presbyterianism in New York State*, ed. and completed by James Hastings Nichols (The Westminster Press, 1963), pp. 117, 119, 122.

20. Drury, *op. cit.*, p. 136.

21. Hayes, *op. cit.*, p. 45.

22. *Ibid.*, pp. 54–56.

23. *Ibid.*, p. 56.

24. *Ibid.*

25. *Ibid.*, p. 53.

26. J. Arthur Lazell, *Alaskan Apostle: The Life Story of Sheldon Jackson* (Harper & Brothers, 1960), p. 35.

27. *Ibid.*, p. 25.

28. *Ibid.*, p. 9.

29. *Ibid.*, p. 56.

30. Drury, *op. cit.*, p. 189.

31. Lazell, *op. cit.*, pp. 174–187.

32. *Rocky Mountain Presbyterian*, February 1873, p. 2.

33. Interview with Miss Edith Agnew, retired missionary to Southwest and missionary biographer, March 31, 1973, in New Mexico.

34. Robert Laird Stewart, *Sheldon Jackson* (Fleming H. Revell, 1908), pp. 257–260.

35. *Rocky Mountain Presbyterian*, May 1873, p. 2.

36. Hayes, *op. cit.*, p. 64.

37. Stewart, *op. cit.*, p. 263.

38. *Rocky Mountain Presbyterian*, February 1873.

39. In an unpublished dissertation, "The Strategy of Sheldon Jackson in Opening the West for National Missions: 1860–1880" (Unpublished Ph.D. dissertation, Graduate School of Yale University, 1948), Alvin Keith Bailey comments on Jackson's remarkable sensitivity to the potentialities of a woman's organization to promote home missions. He quotes from the February 1873 issue of the *Rocky Mountain Presbyterian* these words written by Jackson: "The Ladies' Board of Missions of the Presbyterian Church . . . is the title of an organization for the purpose of enlisting the ladies of the Presbyterian Church more actively in the work of Home and Foreign Missions. . . . But the time has come when they should give more prominence to the Home work" (p. 382).

40. Stewart, *op. cit.*, p. 272.

41. Hayes, *op. cit.*, pp. 72 f.

42. *Ibid.*, pp. 75–77.

43. Drury, *op. cit.*, p. 200.

Chapter 3
"The Women That Publish the Tidings Are a Great Host"

1. M. Katharine Bennett, *A Fiftieth Anniversary*, 1928, pp. 20–21. (Publisher and date unlisted.)

2. Hayes, *op. cit.*, pp. 85–86.
3. *Ibid.*, p. 94.
4. *Ibid.*, p. 103.
5. *Ibid.*, p. 101.
6. Stewart, *op. cit.*, p. 10.
7. Hayes, *op. cit.*, p. 104.
8. *Ibid.*, p. 105.
9. *Ibid.*, pp. 106–108.
10. *Ibid.*, p. 107.
11. *Ibid.*, p. 108.
12. *Ibid.*
13. *Ibid.*, p. 109.
14. *Ibid.*, p. 114.
15. *Minutes of the General Assembly of the Presbyterian Church in the United States of America* (Office of the General Assembly, 1890), p. 43.
16. Hayes, *op. cit.*, p. 113.
17. *Ibid.*, pp. 121–122.
18. *Ibid.*
19. *Ibid.*, p. 123.
20. *Ibid.*, p. 125.
21. Church Women United in the U.S.A., 475 Riverside Drive, New York, N.Y. 10027, is the official sponsor of World Day of Prayer in the United States.
22. Hayes, *op. cit.*, p. 119.
23. *Ibid.*, p. 124.
24. Robert W. Lynn and Elliott Wright, *The Big Little School* (Harper & Row, Publishers, Inc., 1971), p. 57.
25. Hayes, *op. cit.*, p. 124.
26. *Ibid.*, p. 126.
27. Interviews with Miss Jane Gillespie, former Secretary of Specific Work of the Board of National Missions, July 1971, and with Dr. Hermann N. Morse, former General

Secretary of the Board of National Missions, March 1971, both in New York City.

28. Minutes of Woman's Board of Home Missions, June 2, 1914, p. 372.

29. *Ibid.*, Sept. 15, 1914, p. 398.

30. *Ibid.*, Sept. 22, 1914, p. 402.

31. *Ibid.*, p. 403.

32. *Ibid.*

33. *Ibid.*

34. *Ibid.*, Oct. 6, 1914, p. 414.

35. Hayes, *op. cit.*, p. 128.

36. *The Continent*, June 1, 1916. (Publisher unlisted.)

37. Minutes of Woman's Board of Home Missions, Jan. 17, 1922, p. 147.

38. *Ibid.*

39. *Ibid.*, p. 148.

40. *Ibid.*

41. *Ibid.*, p. 149.

42. *Ibid.*, May 2, 1922, p. 28.

43. *Ibid.*, p. 29.

44. *Ibid.*, Oct. 10, 1922, p. 105.

45. Perhaps the concern of the women to preserve their own structure can be more readily understood by the fact that it was a million-dollar-a-year enterprise in which they were involved. In the last year of its existence, the Woman's Board of Home Missions reported:

Receipts:	$1,026,219	for budget items
	41,872	for items outside the budget
	$1,068,091	Total
Relationships:	239,378	members of women's organizations

	182,278 members of young people's groups
	421,656 Presbyterians
Responsibilities:	451 missionaries
	24 boarding schools
	21 day schools
	4,000 pupils
	28 community stations
	18,000 visits to homes
	8 medical centers
	49,000 patients

Areas: Alaska, Orientals on the Pacific Coast, Spanish-speaking people, Indians, Utah, Southern Mountains, Porto Rico, Cuba, Santo Domingo

The above figures appear in *The Home Mission Monthly*, September 1923, p. 253.

46. *Plan of Organization* adopted by the General Assembly in 1923, p. 9.

47. *Ibid.*

48. M. Katharine Bennett, "Mission Agencies in the Presbyterian Church," *Women and Missions*, March 1936, p. 407.

49. *Ibid.*, February 1936, p. 373.

50. At the time of reorganization in 1922–1923, Dr. Hermann N. Morse was the Clerk of the Board of Home Missions; later he became General Secretary of the Board of National Missions.

51. Letter from Dr. Hermann N. Morse dated April 2, 1971.

52. Bennett, "Mission Agencies in the Presbyterian Church," February 1936, p. 373.

53. *The Home Mission Monthly*, June 1923, p. 182.

54. Minutes of the Woman's Board of Home Missions, May 19, 1925, pp. 65 and 111.

55. Selznick, *op. cit.*, p. 14.

Chapter 4
Aftermath and the Drive for Equality

1. *Findings of the Conference on Women's Status and Service in the Church*, St. Paul, Minn., May 20–21, 1929, p. 4. Pamphlet published by General Assembly Publicity Department, Presbyterian Church in the U.S.A.

2. H. Shelton Smith, Robert T. Handy, Lefferts A. Loetscher, *American Christianity 1820–1960* (Charles Scribner's Sons, 1963), Vol. II, p. 220.

3. *Ibid.*

4. Nichols, *op. cit.*, p. 223.

5. *Ibid.*, pp. 218–224.

6. Ernest R. Sandeen, *The Roots of Fundamentalism* (The University of Chicago Press, 1970), p. 232.

7. *Ibid.*, pp. 233–237.

8. *Ibid.*, Introduction, p. ix.

9. *Minutes of the General Assembly*, 1910, pp. 252–253.

10. Nichols, *op. cit.*, p. 218.

11. *Ibid.*, p. 219.

12. Smith, Handy, Loetscher, *op. cit.*, p. 295.

13. Nichols, *op. cit.*, pp. 219–221.

14. *Ibid.*, pp. 221–222.

15. *Ibid.*, p. 222.

16. Smith, Handy, Loetscher, *op. cit.*, p. 345.

17. Robert E. Kofahl, *History and Testimony of the Bible Presbyterian Church*, 3d ed. (Pasadena, Calif.: Highland College, 1965), p. 6.

18. "At the Last Minute," *Women and Missions*, February 1925, p. 442.

19. "Puzzled Over Union," *Women and Missons*, May 1924, p. 75.

20. Miss Margaret Hodge, who had been president of the Woman's Board of Foreign Missions prior to reorganization in 1923, had been elected vice-president of the newly formed Board of Foreign Missions, in much the same way as Mrs. M. Katharine Bennett had become vice-president of the Board of National Missions.

21. Nichols, *op. cit.*, p. 223.

22. M. Katharine Bennett, "Mission Agencies in the Presbyterian Church," *Women and Missions*, April 1936, p. 28.

23. M. Katharine Bennett and Margaret Hodge, *Causes of Unrest Among Women of the Church*, Report to the General Council of the Presbyterian Church in the U.S.A. (1927), p. 9.

24. *Ibid.*

25. *Ibid.*, p. 10.

26. *Ibid.*, pp. 10–11.

27. *Ibid.*, p. 12.

28. *Ibid.*, p. 17.

29. *Ibid.*, p. 25.

30. *Ibid.*, p. 27.

31. Minutes of the Presbytery of Chemung (New York), Vol. IV, p. 401, May 15–16, 1912.

32. *Ibid.*, p. 416.

33. *Ibid.*, pp. 422–423.

34. According to personal knowledge of the author, Miss Rachel Gleason Brooks left the Presbyterian Church and was later ordained by the Congregational Church. She served several pastorates, is now retired and living in Elmira, N.Y. (1972).

35. Minutes of the Presbytery of Chemung, Vol. V (Sept. 24, 1918), pp. 78–79.

36. *Minutes of the General Assembly*, 1919 (Journal), p. 164.

37. Minutes of the Presbytery of Chemung, Vol. V (April 22, 1919), p. 87.

38. *Minutes of the General Assembly*, 1919 (Journal), p. 164.

39. *Minutes of New York Synod*, Oct. 22, 1919, p. 29.

40. *Ibid.*, Oct. 23, 1919, p. 32.

41. *Minutes of the General Assembly*, 1919 (Journal), p. 267.

42. *Ibid.*

43. Minutes of the Presbytery of Chemung, Vol. V (March 23, 1920), p. 105.

44. *Minutes of the General Assembly*, 1920 (Journal), p. 194.

45. *Ibid.*, p. 127.

46. *Minutes of the General Assembly*, 1920 (Journal), p. 127.

47. *Ibid.*, pp. 127–129.

48. *Ibid.*, p. 130.

49. *Ibid.*, p. 131.

50. *Ibid.*, 1921, p. 44.

51. *Ibid.*, 1924, p. 29.

52. *Ibid.*, p. 162.

53. *Ibid.*, 1925, p. 98.

54. *Ibid.*, 1926, p. 33.

55. *Ibid.*, p. 253.

56. *The Relative Place of Women in the Church in the United States:* A Tentative Report of the Joint Committee appointed by the Council of Women for Home Missions, the Federation of Women's Board of Foreign Missions of North America, and the Federal Council of the Churches of Christ in America, to study the place of women's organized work in the church (New York: 1927), p. 10.

57. "General Findings from the Survey of The Relative Place of Women in the Church," April 7, 1927, p. 1.

58. *The Relative Place of Women in the Church*, p. 10.

59. *Ibid.*, p. 53.

60. "General Findings," p. 3.

61. *The Relative Place of Women in the Church*, p. 64.

62. *Ibid.*, p. 13.

63. Minutes of the General Council, Nov. 22, 1928, p. 18.

64. *Ibid.*

65. *Ibid.*

66. *Ibid.*, March 6, 1929, p. 6.

67. *Ibid.*

68. *Ibid.*, p. 7.

69. *Ibid.*, p. 4.

70. *Minutes of the General Assembly*, 1929, pp. 187–191.

71. *Ibid.*

72. *Findings of the Conference on Women's Status and Service in the Church*, p. 4.

73. M. Katharine Bennett and Margaret Hodge, "Overtures on Women Now Before the Church," *The Presbyterian Banner*, Oct. 3, 1929, p. 11.

74. *Ibid.*, p. 27.

75. Clarence E. Macartney, "Shall We Ordain Women as Ministers and Elders?" *The Presbyterian*, Nov. 7, 1929, p. 8.

76. Ethelbert D. Warfield, "May Women Be Ordained in the Presbyterian Church?" *The Presbyterian*, Nov. 14, 1929, p. 6.

77. *Ibid.*

78. *The Presbyterian Banner*, Jan. 16, 1930, p. 32.

79. M. Katharine Bennett, in *Presbyterian Magazine*, Vol. 35, December 1929, p. 624.

80. *Minutes of the General Assembly*, 1930, pp. 52–54.

81. *Ibid.*, 1931, p. 19.

Chapter 5
"Both Men and Women May Be Called to This Office"

1. *The Book of Order, The Constitution of The United Presbyterian Church in the United States of America*, Part II (The Office of the General Assembly of The United Presbyterian Church in the U.S.A., 1967), Form of Government, Ch. VIII, Sec. 2, 38.02.

2. Interview with Dr. Hermann N. Morse in New York City, March 30, 1971.

3. "Women at the General Assembly," *Women and Missions*, July 1930, p. 123.

4. Lynn and Wright, *op. cit.*, pp. 27–32.

5. *Ibid.*, pp. 41–45.

6. *Ibid.*, p. 29.

7. *Ibid.*, pp. 54 f. and 66–68.

8. *Ibid.*, p. 50.

9. *Ibid.*, pp. 78 f.

10. *Ibid.*, p. 80.

11. *Ibid.*, p. 82.

12. *Ibid.*, p. 32.

13. *Ibid.*, p. 84.

14. *Ibid.*, p. 85.

15. *Christian Workers' Bulletin*, Official Publication of the Philadelphia School for Christian Workers of the Presbyterian and Reformed Churches, February 1931, p. 1.

16. *Ibid.*, November 1931, p. 3.

17. *Presbyterian Training School Broadcaster*, Dec. 5, 1928, p. 1.

18. *Ibid.*

19. *School of Religious Education at Auburn Theological Seminary* (First Catalog), Foreword.

20. *Bulletin of Winter Short Courses*, Auburn School of Religious Education, 1923.

21. *Directory of Living Alumni*, Auburn Theological Seminary, March 1948.

22. Letter and questionnaire reply from Mr. Jack McCracken of Evanston, Illinois, dated Aug. 30, 1971.

23. Letters from Miss Dorothy B. Fritz and Miss Neva Palmeter of Santa Fe, N.M., dated July 11 and July 10, 1971, respectively.

24. Letter from Miss Lena Smith of Santa Fe, N.M., dated July 1971, and from Miss Dorothy Arnim of Los Angeles, California, dated August 1971.

25. Letter from Mr. Jack McCracken.

26. *Minutes of the General Assembly*, 1937 (Journal), p. 28.

27. *Ibid.*, 1938, pp. 71–75.

28. *Ibid.*, 1946 (Statistics), pp. 1119 f., and 1956, pp. 689–692.

29. Letter from Mr. Jack McCracken.

30. *Minutes of the General Assembly*, 1943 (Journal), p. 98.

31. *Ibid.*

32. *Ibid.*, 1948 (Journal), pp. 101–102.

33. *Ibid.*, 1949 (Journal), pp. 116–117.

34. Interview with Dr. Ray J. Harmelink, former Associate General Secretary of the Board of Christian Education of The United Presbyterian Church in the U.S.A., in Abington, Pa., on Jan. 8, 1972.

35. *Ibid.*

36. Interview with Dr. W. H. Vernon Smith, former executive of the Board of Christian Education of The United Presbyterian Church in the U.S.A., in New York, N.Y., on Oct. 16, 1971.

37. *Minutes of the General Assembly of the Presbyterian*

Church in the U.S.A. (Annual Report of the Board of Christian Educaton), 1945, p. 55, and 1946, pp. 22–30.

38. *Ibid.*, 1945, pp. 30–31, and 1947, p. 31.

39. *Ibid.*, 1947, p. 68.

40. The author was one of the first four Traveling Fellows appointed by the Board of Christian Education, and served from June 1944 to May 1945.

41. Whenever this happened to me, I indicated my own resentment that the Presbyterian Church still did not ordain women to the ministry, and then proceeded to describe the positive aspects of work in Christian education, such as variety, significance, working with people of all ages, especially young people. Usually, if I thought the girl was particularly well qualified for a church vocation, I shared my conviction that eventually the Presbyterian Church would ordain women as ministers. In fact, to several girls I suggested that if they wanted to go ahead with preparation for ordination, it might be open to them by the time they were ready. If by that time the ministry were still closed to women in the Presbyterian Church, I assured them that they could probably be ordained in the Congregational Church (now United Church of Christ).

In my year's experience as a Traveling Fellow, I do not recall anyone but myself raising the issue concerning the ordination of women. The practice of ordaining only men seemed to be accepted and unquestioned. Whenever I did protest, either in seriousness or in jest, I was made to feel unfeminine, aggressive and difficult, and rebellious by my fellow "Fellows" and by the ministers and others with whom I worked.

42. The author participated in these meetings, 1948–1951.

43. *Minutes of the General Assembly*, 1952 (Journal), p. 35.

44. *Ibid.*

45. *Ibid.*, 1953, p. 99.

46. *Ibid.*, 1954, pp. 106–110.

47. *Ibid.*, 1955, p. 50. During these same years the General Assembly was considering the question of the ordination of women to the ministry.

48. *Ibid.*, 1954, p. 106.

49. *Ibid.*, 1959, p. 64.

50. *Ibid.*

51. *Ibid.*, p. 63.

52. *Ibid.*, p. 58.

53. *Ibid.* (Statistics), 1974, pp. 924–927.

54. *Ibid.* (Journal), 1953, p. 24.

55. *Ibid.*, 1954, pp. 111–112.

56. *Ibid.*, 1955, p. 98.

57. *Ibid.*, 1956, pp. 104–105.

58. Letter from the Rev. C. Vin White of Fremont, Calif., dated Sept. 9, 1971.

59. Letter from the Rev. Frank McCormick of Colorado dated Sept. 10, 1971.

60. Interview with Dr. Hermann N. Morse in New York City on March 30, 1971.

61. This incident was told to the author during the course of several interviews with Miss Margaret Shannon, executive director of Church Women United in the U.S.A., during November 1971.

62. Betty Friedan, *The Feminine Mystique* (Dell Publishing Co., Inc., 1963), pp. 35–44.

Chapter 6
The Rise and Fall of a Power Base

1. Letty M. Russell, *Christian Education in Mission* (The Westminster Press, 1967), p. 24.

2. "Presbyterian Church U.S.A. Ordains First Woman Minister," *Presbyterian Life*, Oct. 27, 1956, p. 18.

3. As a Traveling Fellow of the Board of Christian Education, the author attended this meeting in June 1944.

4. In 1949–50, the author took part in leading several institutes.

5. *The Church Teaches* (Board of Christian Education, The United Presbyterian Church U.S.A., 1964), p. 32.

6. Interview with Dr. W. H. Vernon Smith, June 21, 1973, in New York, N.Y.

7. *Ibid.* These insights have been confirmed by other Christian educators interviewed.

8. Letter from Mr. Jack McCracken, Aug. 30, 1971.

9. Interview with Mr. Hamlin Tobey, Nov. 25, 1973.

10. *Ibid.* This fact has been corroborated by many other directors of Christian education, as well as by personal knowledge of the author who attended 1948–1951.

11. List of "Charter Members of NADCE" compiled by the Board of Christian Education, dated Nov. 20, 1958.

12. Interview with W. H. Vernon Smith, June 21, 1973.

13. *Ibid.*

14. Through its Presbyterian societies, the Presbyterian Women's Organization in 1954 contributed $3,383,311 to the general mission budget, or 24.6 percent of the total, $13,725,215.

15. This is speculation based on numerous conversations with Christian educators during the period 1946–1966.

16. List of registrants for the NADCE meeting held on Feb. 7–8, 1959, in Omaha, Nebr., prepared by the Board of Christian Education.

17. Interview with W. H. Vernon Smith, June 21, 1973, and corroborated by Hamlin Tobey and others. Membership lists unavailable.

18. List of officers on the letterhead of the Association of Presbyterian Christian Educators (APCE) for 1972.

19. In checking 125 of the 1963 Annual Reports from congregations (out of approximately 9,000), the author found that the information given is not reliable, even if it were available. Some churches with memberships of under 1,000 reported having a director of Christian education *and* an assistant in Christian education, with the same person listed as church school superintendent or junior high teacher, etc. An additional source of information would have been the special section added to the Annual Report of congregations every four years, beginning in 1963, which requested further information about Christian education personnel. These special sections were returned to the Office of Vocation in the former Board of Christian Education. These forms, however, were destroyed after they were used by that office in 1963 and 1967; in 1971 the computer did not work properly and the reports were never completed.

20. Churches of fewer than 500 members rarely employ a second staff person with responsibility for Christian education.

21. To maintain the confidentiality of these comments, no identification is listed.

22. The General Assembly appointed a Special Committee on the Nature of the Ministry in 1958; the final report of that committee was made in 1965.

23. Harriet Prichard, "Some Practical Reflections on 'The Nature of the Ministry' Report" (unpublished, in ditto form), pp. 4–5.

24. *Ibid.*, p. 11.

25. From a "Memo to a group of selected respondents to the questionnaire circulated in May 1965 about TAUPCE's study on 'The Nature of the Ministry,' " p. 18.

26. Interview with Dr. Frederick Maier, formerly head of the Institute of Strategic Studies of the Board of National Missions, in New York City, on Dec. 12, 1972.

27. Proposals to this effect were discussed at the meeting of TAUPCE attended by the author in Dallas, Tex., February 1970.

28. Friedan, *op. cit.*

29. Selznick, *op. cit.*, p. 261.

30. Interviews with W. H. Vernon Smith, Hamlin Tobey, William Henderson, Edith Agnew, Miriam Jones, Elizabeth McCort.

Chapter 7
"In Christ There Is Neither Male nor Female" . . . But in the Presbyterian Church?

1. Drury, *op. cit.*, p. 209.
2. *Ibid.*, p. 210.
3. *Ibid.*, pp. 206–207.
4. *Ibid.*, pp. 205–210, and Hayes, *op. cit.*, pp. 129–131.
5. Selznick, *op. cit.*, p. 13.
6. *Ibid.*
7. *Ibid.*
8. *Ibid.*, p. 261.
9. *Ibid.*
10. Carl Jung, *The Archetypes and The Collective Unconscious* (Princeton University Press, 1959), Collected Works, Vol. IX, Pt. 1, pp. 42 f.
11. The Reformed Church in America ordained its first woman minister, the Rev. Joyce Stedge, on Oct. 7, 1973, in Spring Valley, N.Y., with the author in attendance at the service.
12. Joseph Rheingold, *The Fear of Being a Woman* (Grune & Stratton, Inc., 1964), p. 212.

13. Sigmund Freud, *New Introductory Lectures on Psychoanalysis* (W. W. Norton & Company, Inc., 1965), p. 128.

14. Karen Horney, *Feminine Psychology* (W. W. Norton & Company, Inc., 1967), pp. 158 ff.

15. Erik Erikson, "Reflections on Womanhood," in Robert Jay Lifton (ed.), *The Woman in America* (Houghton Mifflin Company, 1965), p. 6.

16. Otto Rank, *Beyond Psychology* (Dover Publications, Inc., 1941), p. 256.

17. *Ibid.*, p. 259.

18. *Ibid.*

19. Carl Jung, *Two Essays on Analytical Psychology* (Meridian Books, Inc., 1956), pp. 218–221.

20. Paul Tournier attributes the greater response of women to church life to a difference in conscience. He states: "The man who is dishonest in business cannot go to church, cannot hear the law of the gospel, without feeling discomfort. A woman, on the other hand, who is jealous or who detests her daughter-in-law, can listen to and even approve a sermon on love without any feeling of embarrassment." (*The Whole Person in a Broken World* [Harper & Row, Publishers, Inc., 1964], p. 17.)

21. Kathleen Bliss, *The Service and Status of Women in Churches* (London: SCM Press, Ltd., 1952), p. 183.

22. William L. O'Neil, *Everyone Was Brave: The Rise and Fall of Feminism in America* (Quadrangle Books, Inc., 1969), p. 351.

23. *Ibid.*, p. 352.

24. *Ibid.*, p. 355.

25. In any discussion of the power cycle, it must be remembered that there are other dimensions involved in the relationships that affect its operation. For example, male clergy have often been considered somewhat ineffectual as persons—less aggressive, more conciliatory and compassion-

ate, whereas women parishioners have frequently been extremely able leaders—aggressive, innovative, diligent. Strong churchwomen, then, have found themselves in the position of being powerless within the church *structure*, with vapid clergymen holding the reins of power. It is a case of the "powerless" being in power and the "powerful" being out of power. Is this perhaps one factor that might account for the love-hate relationship that sometimes exists between male clergymen and women parishioners?

Selected Bibliography

Books

Bliss, Kathleen. *The Service and Status of Women in the Churches.* London: SCM Press, Ltd., 1952.

The Book of Order, The Constitution of The United Presbyterian Church in the United States of America, Part II. The Office of the General Assembly of The United Presbyterian Church in the U.S.A., 1967.

Doeley, Sarah B. (ed.). *Women's Liberation and the Church.* Association Press, 1970.

Drury, Clifford M. *Presbyterian Panorama.* The Westminster Press, 1952.

Erikson, Erik. "Reflections on Womanhood," in Robert Jay Lifton (ed.), *The Woman in America.* Houghton Mifflin Company, 1965.

Flexner, Eleanor. *Century of Struggle: The Woman's Rights Movement in the United States.* The Belknap Press of Harvard University Press, 1959.

Freud, Sigmund. *New Introductory Lectures on Psychoanalysis*. W. W. Norton & Company, Inc., 1965.

Friedan, Betty. *The Feminine Mystique*. Dell Publishing Co., Inc., 1963.

Gage, Matilda Joslyn. *Woman, Church and State*. C. H. Kerr and Co., 1893.

Hayes, Florence. *Daughters of Dorcas*. Board of National Missions, Presbyterian Church in the U.S.A., 1952.

Horney, Karen. *Feminine Psychology*. W. W. Norton & Company, Inc., 1967.

Hummel, Margaret Gibson, and Roe, Mildred. *The Amazing Heritage*. The Geneva Press, 1970.

Jencks, Christopher, and Riesman, David. *The Academic Revolution*. Doubleday & Company, Inc., 1968.

Jung, Carl. *The Archetypes and The Collective Unconscious*, Collected Works, Vol. IX, Pt. 1. Princeton University Press, 1969.

―――― *The Basic Writings of C. G. Jung*, ed. by Violet Staub de Laszlo. Modern Library, Inc., 1959.

―――― *Two Essays on Analytical Psychology*. Meridian Books, Inc., 1956.

Lazell, J. Arthur. *Alaskan Apostle: The Life Story of Sheldon Jackson*. Harper & Brothers, 1960.

Lynn, Robert W., and Wright, Elliott. *The Big Little School*. Harper & Row, Publishers, Inc., 1971.

Nichols, Robert Hastings. *Presbyterianism in New York State*, ed. and completed by James Hastings Nichols. The Westminster Press, 1963.

Notable American Women: 1607–1950, Vol. III. The Belknap Press of the Harvard University Press, 1971.

O'Neil, William L. *Everyone Was Brave: The Rise and Fall of Feminism in America*. Quadrangle Books, Inc., 1969.

The Presbyterian Constitution and Digest, Vol. I. Published

for the Office of the General Assembly by the Board of Christian Education, Presbyterian Church in the U.S.A., 1956.
Rank, Otto. *Beyond Psychology*. Dover Publications, Inc., 1941.
Rheingold, Joseph. *The Fear of Being a Woman*. Grune & Stratton, Inc., 1964.
Russell, Letty M. *Christian Education in Mission*. The Westminster Press, 1967.
Sandeen, Ernest R. *The Roots of Fundamentalism*. The University of Chicago Press, 1970.
Selznick, Philip. *TVA and the Grass Roots*. University of California Publications in Culture and Society, Vol. III. University of California Press, 1949.
Smith, H. Shelton; Handy, Robert T.; and Loetscher, Lefferts A. *American Christianity 1820–1960*, Vol. II. Charles Scribner's Sons, 1963.
Stanton, Elizabeth Cady. *Eighty Years and More: Reminiscences, 1818–1897*. Reprinted from the T. Fisher Unwin edition of 1898; Shocken Books, 1971.
Stewart, Robert Laird. *Sheldon Jackson*. Fleming H. Revell, 1908.
Terkel, Studs. *Hard Times: An Oral History of the Great Depression*. Avon Books, 1970.
Thompson, Robert E. *A History of the Presbyterian Churches in the U.S.* The Christian Literature Co., 1895.
Tournier, Paul. *The Whole Person in a Broken World*. Harper & Row, Publishers, Inc., 1964.

REFERENCE WORKS

Dictionary of American Biography. Vols. VII and XVII. Charles Scribner's Sons, 1935.

The Random House College Dictionary. Random House, Inc., 1968.

The Random House Dictionary of the English Language (Unabridged). Random House, Inc., 1966.

Webster's Seventh New Collegiate Dictionary. G. & C. Merriam Company, 1963.

Articles and Periodicals

"A Wonderful Year," *Women and Missions*, June 1924.

"At the Last Minute," *Women and Missions*, February 1925.

Bennett, M. Katharine. "Mission Agencies in the Presbyterian Church," *Women and Missions*, February 1936. Also March 1936 and April 1936.

——— "Why These Overtures?" *Presbyterian Magazine*, December 1929.

——— and Hodge, Margaret. "Overtures on Women Now Before the Church," *The Presbyterian Banner*, Oct. 3, 1929.

Cole, Doris. "Women—Church Members Second Class," *Vanguard*, A Bulletin for Church Officers. Board of Christian Education, The United Presbyterian Church U.S.A. Vol. IV, No. 3 (May 1967).

The Continent, June 1, 1916. Newspaper clipping found in the Board of National Missions, Interchurch Center, 475 Riverside Drive, New York, N.Y., in 1972.

Dawson, Lucy. "A Going Concern," *The Home Mission Monthly*, September 1923.

The Home Mission Monthly, September 1923 and June 1923.

McAfee, Cleland B. "Women and Official Church Life," *The Presbyterian Banner*, Jan. 16, 1930.

Macartney, Clarence E. "Shall We Ordain Women as Ministers and Elders?" *The Presbyterian*, Nov. 7, 1929.

Pikrone, Mary Anne. "Her Trying Hour Before Assembly," *The Times-Union*, Rochester, N.Y., May 25, 1971.

"Presbyterian Church U.S.A. Ordains First Woman Minister," *Presbyterian Life*, Oct. 27, 1956.

"Puzzled Over Union," *Women and Missions*, May 1924.

Rice, Betty M. "Report of Meeting on 'Women and Church,'" *Christianity and Crisis*, Vol. XI, No. 14 (Aug. 6, 1951).

Rocky Mountain Presbyterian, February and May 1873.

Warfield, Ethelbert D. "May Women Be Ordained in the Presbyterian Church?" *The Presbyterian*, Nov. 14, 1929.

Way, Peggy. "Women in the Church," *Renewal*, Vol. IV, No. 7 (October 1964).

"Women at the General Assembly," *Women and Missions*, July 1930.

Pamphlets and Reports

Bennett, M. Katharine. *A Fiftieth Anniversary*. Publisher and date unlisted.

——— and Hodge, Margaret. *Causes of Unrest Among Women of the Church*. Report to the General Council of the Presbyterian Church in the U.S.A., 1927.

Bulletin of Winter Short Courses. Auburn School of Religious Education, Auburn, N.Y., 1923.

Christian Workers' Bulletin. Official publication of the Philadelphia School for Christian Workers of the Presbyterian and Reformed Churches, February 1931 and November 1931.

The Church Teaches. Board of Christian Education, The United Presbyterian Church U.S.A., 1964.

Directory of Living Alumni. Auburn Theological Seminary, March 1948.

Federal Council of the Churches of Christ in America. *The Relative Place of Women in the Church in the United States.* A tentative report of the Joint Committee appointed by the Council of Women for Home Missions, the Federation of Women's Boards of Foreign Missions of North America, and the Federal Council of the Churches of Christ in America. New York, 1927.

Findings of the Conference on Women's Status and Service in the Church, St. Paul, Minn., May 20–21, 1929. General Assembly Publicity Department, Presbyterian Church in the U.S.A.

Hays, George P. *May Women Speak?* Women's Temperance Publication Association, 1889.

Kofahl, Robert E. *History and Testimony of the Bible Presbyterian Church.* 3d ed. Pasadena, Calif.: Highland College, 1965.

New York Synod. *Minutes of New York Synod.* 1919.

Plan of Organization. The Office of the General Assembly of the Presbyterian Church in the U.S.A., 1923.

Presbyterian Historical Society. The 1963 Annual Reports to the General Assembly (Official Body) from Congregations of The United Presbyterian Church in the U.S.A.

Presbyterian Training School Broadcaster, Dec. 5, 1928.

Religious Education Association. *Proceedings of the First Convention of the Religious Education Association.* Chicago, 1903.

Report of the Special Committee on the Nature of the Ministry to the General Assembly of The United Presbyterian Church in the U.S.A., 1965.

School of Religious Education at Auburn Theological Seminary, First Catalog. Union Theological Seminary. New York, N.Y.

Task Force on the Status of Women. *Summary of Question-*

naires from 35 Ordained Women of the United Presbyterian Church. 1970.

Tennent College Bulletin, November 1932.

The United Presbyterian Church in the U.S.A. *Minutes of the General Assembly.* The Office of the General Assembly, 1803–1811, 1890, 1903, 1910, 1919–1921, 1924–1926, 1929–1931, 1937–1938, 1943–1946, 1952–1971, 1974.

UNPUBLISHED MATERIAL

Arnim, Dorothy. Letter received from Los Angeles, Calif., dated August 1971.

Bailey, Alvin Keith. "The Strategy of Sheldon Jackson in Opening the West for National Missions: 1860–1880." Unpublished Ph.D. dissertation, Graduate School of Yale University, 1948.

Covenant Presbyterian Church, Columbus, Ohio. Letter to Miss Winsome Munro of New York, May 10, 1971.

Fritz, Dorothy B. Letter received from Santa Fe, N. Mex., dated July 11, 1971.

General Assembly Special Committee on the Nature of the Ministry. Minutes of meetings 1958–1965. Mimeographed.

General Council of the Presbyterian Church U.S.A. Minutes of the General Council, Nov. 30, 1927; May 22–23, 1928; Nov. 22, 1928; March 6, 1929; October 1937.

"General Findings from the Survey of The Relative Place of Women in the Church," April 7, 1927. Mimeographed.

Henderson, William H. "The Professional Ministry of the United Presbyterian Church." Reports prepared for the Office of Vocation, Board of Christian Education of The United Presbyterian Church in the U.S.A., 1970 and 1971.

McCormick, Frank. Letter dated Sept. 10, 1971.

McCracken, Jack. Letter received from Evanston, Ill., dated Aug. 30, 1971.

McCullogh, Kenneth G. "Observations from Employment Records of Ordained United Presbyterian Women," Task Force on Women in the Church, The United Presbyterian Church U.S.A., 1969.

"Memo to a group of selected respondents to the questionnaire circulated in May 1965 about TAUPCE's study on 'The Nature of the Ministry.'" Mimeographed.

Morse, Hermann N. Letter dated April 2, 1971.

Mudge, Lewis S. Telegram to the Rev. Mark Matthews of Seattle, Wash., dated April 4, 1929.

National Association of Directors of Christian Education. List of registrants for the meeting held Feb. 7–8, 1959, in Omaha, Nebr., prepared for Hamlin Tobey of the Board of Christian Education, Philadelphia. Typewritten.

Naylor, Natalie Ann. "Raising a Learned Ministry: The American Education Society, 1815–1860." Unpublished Ed.D. dissertation, Teachers College, Columbia University, New York, N.Y., 1971.

Palmeter, Neva. Letter received from Santa Fe, N. Mex., dated July 10, 1971.

Presbytery of Chemung (New York). Minutes of meetings. Vols. IV and V, 1918–1920.

Prichard, Harriet. Letter from Sunland, Calif., dated June 11, 1972.

——— "Some Practical Reflections on 'The Nature of the Ministry' Report." Ditto form.

Smith, Lena. Letter received from Santa Fe, N. Mex., dated July 1971.

Vocation Agency, The United Presbyterian Church U.S.A. "Ordained Women in the United Presbyterian Church."

Report prepared by the Office of Enlistment, Candidates, and Career Counseling. January 1973.

White, C. Vin. Letter received from Fremont, Calif., dated Sept. 9, 1971.

Woman's Board of Home Missions. Minutes of the Board, May 7, 1912; Jan. 17, 1922; June 12, 1925; and May 19, 1925.

Woman's Board of Home Missions. Minutes of the Executive Committee, April 27, 1915.

Woman's Board of Home Missions. Minutes of the Board and Executive Committee, May 7, 1912; June 2, 1914; Sept. 15, 1914; Sept. 22, 1914; Oct. 6, 1914; Jan. 5, 1915; March 2, 1915; April 27, 1915; Jan. 17, 1922; May 2, 1922; Oct. 10, 1922; Oct. 31, 1922; May 19, 1925; June 12, 1925.

Other Sources

Agnew, Edith, retired missionary to the Southwest and missionary biographer. Personal interview in Santa Fe, N. Mex., March 31, 1973.

Gillespie, Jane, former Secretary for Specific Work of the Board of National Missions of The United Presbyterian Church in the U.S.A. Personal interview in New York, N.Y., July 12, 1971.

Harmelink, Ray J., former Associate General Secretary of the Board of Christian Education of The United Presbyterian Church in the U.S.A. Personal interview in Abington, Pa., Jan. 8, 1972.

Maier, Frederick, director of the Institute of Strategic Studies of the Board of National Missions of The United Presbyterian Church in the U.S.A. Personal interview in New York, N.Y., Dec. 12, 1972.

Morse, Hermann N., former General Secretary of the Board of National Missions of The United Presbyterian Church in the U.S.A. Personal interview in New York, N.Y., March 30, 1971.

Professional Women's Caucus and one member of the Permanent Judicial Commission of the General Assembly of The United Presbyterian Church in the U.S.A. Informal meeting in the Rochester War Memorial Auditorium, Rochester, N.Y., May 25, 1971.

Shannon, Margaret, executive director of Church Women United in the U.S.A. Personal interviews in New York, N.Y., November and December 1971.

Smith, W. H. Vernon, former executive with the Board of Christian Education of The United Presbyterian Church in the U.S.A. Personal interviews in New York, N.Y., Oct. 16, 1972, and June 21, 1973.

Stair, Lois, Moderator of the 184th General Assembly of The United Presbyterian Church in the U.S.A. Personal interview at Gustavus Adolphus College, St. Peter, Minn., July 26, 1972.

Tobey, Hamlin, former executive with the Board of Christian Education of The United Presbyterian Church in the U.S.A., and Mrs. Kathrene Tobey, professional Christian educator and author. Telephone interview from Garnerville, N.Y., to Sharon, Conn., Nov. 25, 1973.